Introduction

✓ *Are you always looking for easier and more modern ways to bake the best cakes for you and all your loved ones?*

✓ *Are you constantly looking for simpler and more time-saving recipes with available kitchen appliances?*

Well, you don't need to search anymore!
We present to you today the best.

First of all, you need to know that air fryers are special and revolutionary kitchen appliances that cook your food using the circulation of hot air. All the food you cook in these fryers is succulent on the inside and perfectly cooked on the outside.
They allow you to cook , bake, steam and roast pretty much everything you can imagine, help you cook your meals in a much healthier way. So many people all over the world just fell in love with this great and amazing tool and now it's your turn to become one of them.

This every cakes recipes collection will show you how to make the best breakfasts, side dishes, snacks, the best desserts.

What could be more wonderful than you can make some cakes for your loved ones to enjoy on the occasion of a certain holiday? Especially with this book, the time to make cakes will be shorter and more convenient when simply baking in an air fryer?

So, let's get started!
Have fun cooking with your great kitchen!

Table of Content

BREAD

Pineapple Squash Bread	2
Buttermilk Bread	3
Muffin Breakfast Sandwich	4
Banana Bread	5
Banana Nut Bread	6
Apple Bread	7
Air Fried Sandwich	8
Cheesy Breakfast Bread	9
Breakfast Bread Pudding	10
Potato Bread Rolls	11

CAKE

Chocolate Cake	13
Lime Cheesecake	14
Strawberry Cream Cake	15
Cranberry Cakes	16
Coffee Cheesecakes	17
Poppyseed Cake	18
Lemon Pound Cake	19
Carrot Cake	20
Orange Cake	21
Sponge Cake	22
Ricotta and Lemon Cake	23
Tangerine Cake	24
Strawberry Shortcakes	25
Tomato Cake	26
Black Tea Cake	27
Plum Cake	28

CAKE

Chocolate Sponge Cake	29
Maple Cupcakes	30
Mini Chocolate Peanut Butter Cupcakes.	31
Strawberry Cupcakes	32
Chocolate Souffle	33
Molten Chocolate Cakes	34
Upside Down Pineapple Cake	35
Sweet Potato Cheesecake	36
Cardamom Cakes	37
Stuffed French Toast	38
Crunchy French Toast	39
Simple Pancakes	40
Honey and Orange Pancakes	41
Zucchini Pancakes	42
Pumpkin Pancakes	43
Grilled Cheese	44
Triple Berry Turnovers	45
Mushroom Cakes	46
Cauliflower Cakes	47

MUFFIN

Egg Muffins	49
Cheese Corn Muffins	50
Blueberry Muffins	51
Pumpkin Muffins	52
Coffee Streusel Muffins	53
Oats Muffins	54

Table of Content

MUFFIN

Blueberry Lemon Muffins	55
Orange Cranberry Muffins	56
Chocolate Chip Muffins	57
Chocolate Espresso Muffins	58
Banana Nut Muffins	59
Banana Muffins	60
Cheesy Cornbread Muffins	61
Chocolate Muffins	62

DONUTS

Simple Donuts	64
Strawberry Donuts	65
Everything Bagels	66
Oreo Mini Donuts	67
Vanilla Mini Donuts	68
Cinnamon Sugar Donuts	69

COOKIES

Macaroons	71
Coconut Macaroons	72
Honey and Oats Cookie	73
Danisa Cookie	74
Cookie Custards	75
Brown Butter Cookies	76
Pignoli Cookies	77
Pumpkin Cookies	78
Tasty Orange Cookies	79
Chocolate Chip Cookies	80
Lentils Cookies	81
Lentils and Dates Brownies	82
Vanilla Brownies	83
Fudgy Gluten-Free Brownies	84

PIE, BISCUITS, TARTS & MORE

Strawberry Pie	86
Pumpkin Pie	87
Coconut Hand Pies	88
Chicken Pie	89
Ham Breakfast Pie	90
Peach Pie	91
Mini Apple Pies	92
Cinnamon Sugar Churros	93
Cheese Crackers	94
Mushrooms Stuffed	95
Cheddar Biscuits	96
Biscuits Casserole	97
Buttermilk Biscuits	98
Simple Potato Chips	99
Sweet Potato Chips	100
Tasty Cinnamon Toast	101
Strawberry Jam Tarts	102
Chocolate Tarts	103
Blueberry Tarts	104
Fruit Tarts	105
Lemon Tart	106
Blueberry Pop Tart	107
Plum and Currant Tart	109

BREAD

Pineapple Squash Bread

1 Medium Loaf or 3 Mini Loaves | 25 minutes

INGREDIENTS

- 275 grams Strong bread flour.
- 1 1/2 tsp Instant dry yeast.
- 2 tbsp Warm water.
- 250 grams Squash puree.
- 1/4 tsp Chili powder.
- 1/2 tsp Salt.
- 1 tbsp Olive oil.
- 1/2 tbsp Curry powder.
- 1 tbsp Cumin.

DIRECTIONS

1. Whisk together warm water and yeast with a mixer. Let stand for 10 minutes to create foam.
2. Mix the squash puree into the flour until it resembles fine breadcrumbs. When yeast is ready, put flour into the bowl and add salt, spices, and oil.
3. Mix and knead until the dough is soft and elastic.
4. Transfer dough into an oiled bowl and let it stand to rise for 1 hour or until doubled in size.
5. Sprinkle flour into loaf tins. Knead the dough again briefly this time with the pineapple chunks and form into a loaf shape. Let stand for 1 hour.
6. Preheat Instant Air Fryer to 190oC.
7. Bake the loaf for 25 minutes.

Buttermilk Bread

INGREDIENTS

- All-purpose flour 300 gr
- Fresh milk without sugar 60 ml
- Unsalted Butter 50 gr
- Instant yeast 5 gr
- Salt 1/4 teaspoon
- Sugar 2 tablespoons
- 1 chicken egg

DIRECTIONS

1. Put 300g of all-purpose flour and 5g of yeast in a bowl, mix well. Add 1/4 teaspoon of salt, 2 tablespoons of sugar, add 1 egg and 60ml of fresh milk, mix well again. (Note about yeast: Put the salt and yeast at a distance from each other, if the yeast comes into direct contact with the salt, the yeast will die)
2. Take the dough out and start kneading the dough. First you fold the dough, then use the back of your hand, press and rub, push the dough away (Folding and Stretching). Note that pressing and spreading the dough away, not down. Rotate the dough 90 degrees, repeat the two steps above.
3. After kneading for about 10-15 minutes, add 50g of unsalted butter and dried cranberries and continue kneading.
4. Knead until the butter is incorporated into the dough, the dough becomes soft, chewy, smooth and does not stick to your hands. Break the dough out and pull it into a thin film. Cover the dough with cling film and leave for about 45 minutes in the refrigerator to double in size.
5. Divide the dough into equal portions according to the size of your pan. Cover the dough and let it rest for about 10 minutes before shaping.
6. You can mold into circles, spirals or as long as you like. Cover the dough and let it rest for about 15 minutes before baking.
7. Line a sheet of foil in the tray of the air fryer, heat the pot at 160 degrees for about 3 minutes.
8. Place the cake in the pan. Bake the cake at about 160 degrees Celsius for 5 minutes, then open the pot, turn the cake and bake for about 5 more minutes until the cake is cooked evenly.
9. Let the Bread cool and serve.

Muffin Breakfast Sandwich

Serving: 1   15 minutes

DIRECTIONS

- 1 English muffin, halved.
- 1 slice white cheddar cheese.
- 1 slice Canadian bacon.
- 1 tablespoon hot water.
- 1 large egg Salt & pepper, to taste.
- Cooking spray.

Items needed: 1 (3-ounce) rameki

INGREDIENTS

1. Spray the inside of the ramekin with cooking spray and place it into the Air Fryer.
2. Preheat the Air Fryer in temperature to 320°F.
3. Add the cheese and Canadian bacon to 1 half of the English muffin.
4. Place both halves of the muffin into the preheated air fryer. Then pour the hot water and egg into the heated ramekin and season with salt and pepper. Bake for 10 minutes
5. Take the English muffins out after 7 minutes, but leave the egg for the full time.
6. Assemble your sandwich by placing the cooked egg on top of the English muffin, then serve.

Banana Bread

Serving: 6   50 minutes

INGREDIENTS

- 2 bananas, mashed.
- ¾ cup sugar.
- 1 teaspoon vanilla extract.
- 1/3 cup butter.
- 1.5 cups flour.
- 1 egg.
- 1 teaspoon baking powder.
- ½ teaspoons baking soda.
- 1/3 cup milk.
- 1.5 teaspoons cream of tartar.
- Cooking spray.

DIRECTIONS

1. Mix milk with cream of tartar, sugar, butter, egg, vanilla and bananas In a bowl and stir everything.
2. In second bowl, mix flour with baking powder and baking soda.
3. Combine the 2 above mixtures, stir well, pour this into a cake pan greased with some cooking spray.
4. Introduce in your air fryer and cook at 320 degrees F for 38-40 minutes.
5. Take bread out, leave aside to cool down, slice and serve it.

Banana Nut Bread

🍴 1 Medium Loaf   🕐 50 minutes

INGREDIENTS

- 1 egg.
- 1/2 cup sugar.
- 1/4 cup unsalted butter, softened.
- 2 overripe bananas, mashed.
- 1/4 teaspoon vanilla extract.
- 1/2 teaspoon baking soda.
- 1/2 cup chopped walnuts.
- 3/4 cups all-purpose flour
- 1/2 teaspoon salt.
- Cooking spray.

Items needed: 1 mini loaf pan

DIRECTIONS

1. Mix Cream together the butter and sugar. Then add egg, mashed bananas, and vanilla extract until well combined. Set aside.
2. Preheat the Air Fryer, adjust temperature to 300°F.
3. Sift together the flour, baking soda, and salt.
4. Fold the dry ingredients into the wet until combined. Mix in the chopped walnuts.
5. Grease the mini loaf pan with cooking spray, then fill with batter. Place into the preheated air fryer.
6. Select the Bake function, adjust time to 40 minutes.
7. Done and serve.

Apple Bread

Serving: 6   50 minutes

INGREDIENTS

- 2 eggs.
- 3 cups apples, cored and cubed.
- 1 tablespoon apple pie spice.
- 1 cup sugar.
- 2 cups white flour.
- 1 tablespoon vanilla.
- 1 stick butter.
- 1 tablespoon baking powder.
- 1 cup water.

DIRECTIONS

1. Mix egg with 1 butter stick, apple pie spice and sugar in a bowl and stir using mixer.
2. Add apples to the above mixture and stir again well.
3. In second bowl, mix baking powder with flour and stir.
4. Combine the 2 mixtures, stir and pour into a spring form pan.
5. Put spring form pan in your air fryer and cook at 320 degrees F for 40 minutes.
6. Slice and serve.

Air Fried Sandwich

Servings: 2   10 minutes

INGREDIENTS

- 2 English muffins, halved.
- 2 bacon strips
- 2 eggs
- Salt and black pepper to the taste

DIRECTIONS

1. Crack eggs in your air fryer, add bacon on top, cover and cook at 392 degrees F for 6 minutes.
2. Heat up your English muffin halves in your microwave for a few seconds, divide eggs on 2 halves, add bacon on top, season with salt and pepper, cover with the other 2 English muffins and serve.

Cheesy Breakfast Bread

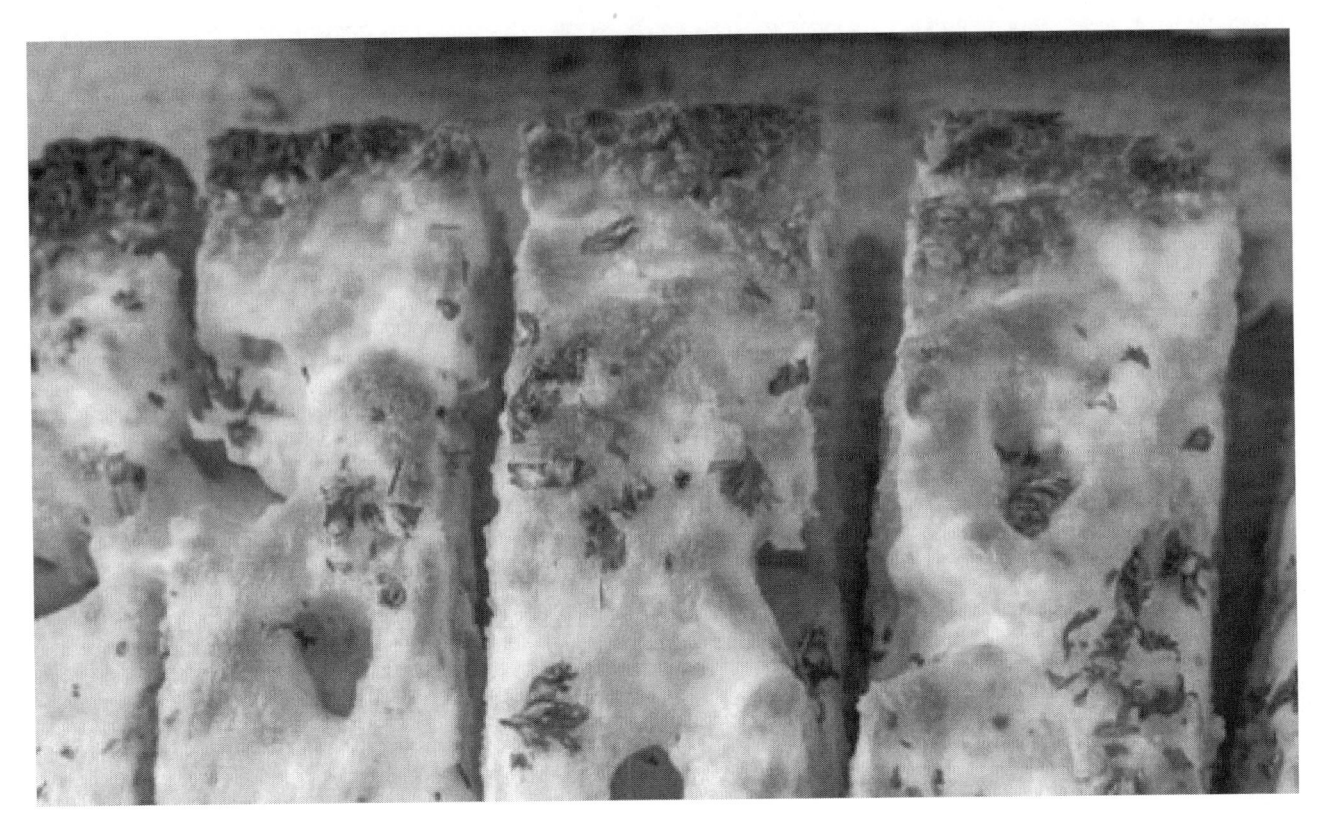

Servings: 4   10 minutes

INGREDIENTS

- 6 bread slices.
- 3 garlic cloves, minced.
- 1 cup mozzarella cheese, grate.
- 5 tablespoons butter melted.
- 6 teaspoons sun dried tomato pesto.

DIRECTIONS

1. Arrange bread slices on a surface.
2. Spread butter all over, divide tomato paste, garlic and top with grated cheese.
3. Add bread slices to your heated air fryer and cook them at 350 degrees F for 8 minutes.
4. Divide among plates and serve.

Breakfast Bread Pudding

Servings: 4   22 minutes

INGREDIENTS

- 1/2 pound white bread, cubed.
- 3 ounces soft butter.
- 3/4 cup milk.
- 2 teaspoons cornstarch.
- 3/4 cup water.
- 5 tablespoons honey.
- 1/2 cup apple, peeled, cored and roughly chopped.
- 2 teaspoons cinnamon powder.
- 1 teaspoon vanilla extract.
- 0.6 cup brown sugar.
- 1,3 cup flour.

DIRECTIONS

1. Mix bread with apple, milk with water, honey, cinnamon, vanilla and cornstarch and beat well in a bowl.
2. In another bowl, mix flour with sugar and butter and stir until you obtain a crumbled mixture.
3. Preheat the air fryer to 350 degrees F for 3 minutes.
4. Press half of the crumble mix on the bottom of your air fryer, add bread and apple mix, add the rest of the crumble and cook everything at 350 degrees F for 20-22 minutes.
5. Divide bread pudding on plates and serve.

Potato Bread Rolls

Servings: 4   20 minutes

INGREDIENTS

- 5 potatoes, boiled, peeled and mashed.
- 2 tablespoons olive oil Salt and black pepper to the taste.
- 8 bread slices, white parts only.
- ½ teaspoon mustard seeds
- 1 coriander bunch, chopped.
- 2 small yellow onions, chopped.
- 2 green chilies, chopped.
- 2 curry leaf springs.
- ½ teaspoon turmeric powder.

DIRECTIONS

1. Heat up a pan with 1 tsp oil, add mustard seeds, curry leaves, onions and turmeric, stir and cook for a few seconds.
2. Add mashed potatoes, pepper, salt, coriander and chilies, stir well, take off heat and cool it down.
3. Divide potatoes mix into 8 parts and shape ovals using your wet hands.
4. Wet bread slices with water, press in order to drain excess water and keep one slice in your palm.
5. Add a potato oval over bread slice and wrap it around it.
6. Repeat with the rest of the potato mix and bread.
7. Heat up your air fryer at 400 degrees F, add the rest of the oil, add bread rolls, cook them for 12 minutes.

CAKE

Chocolate Cake

Servings: 12   40 minutes

INGREDIENTS

- 1 egg.
- 1 banana, mashed.
- 3/4 cup white flour.
- 3/4 teaspoon pumpkin pie spice.
- 3/4 cup whole wheat flour.
- 1 teaspoon baking soda.
- 8 ounces canned pumpkin puree.
- 3/4 cup sugar.
- 2/3 cup chocolate chips.
- 1/2 teaspoon baking powder.
- 1/2 teaspoon vanilla extract.
- 2 tablespoons canola oil.
- 1/2 cup Greek yogurt.
- Cooking spray.

DIRECTIONS

1. Mix white flour with whole wheat flour, salt, baking soda and powder and pumpkin spice in a bowl and stir.
2. In another bowl, mix sugar with oil, banana, yogurt, pumpkin puree, vanilla and egg and stir using a mixer.
3. Combine the 2 mixtures, add chocolate chips, stir, pour this into a greased Bundt pan. (Note to choose the Bundt pan that is the right size for the air fryer)
4. Introduce in your air fryer and bake at 330 degrees F for 30 minutes.
5. Leave the cake to cool down, before cutting and serving it.

Lime Cheesecake

Servings: 12   40 minutes

INGREDIENTS

- 2 tablespoons butter, melted.
- 1/4 cup coconut, shredded.
- 2 teaspoons sugar.
- 4 ounces flour.

The filling:
- 1 pound cream cheese.
- 2 sachets lime jelly.
- Grated Juice form 1 lime.
- Zest from 1 lime,
- 2 cups hot water.

DIRECTIONS

1. Mix coconut with flour, butter and sugar in a bowl, stir well and put this on the bottom of a pan that fits your air fryer.
2. Meanwhile, put the hot water in another bowl, add jelly sachets and stir until it dissolves.
3. Put cream cheese in a bowl, add jelly, lime juice and zest and whisk really well.
4. Add this over the crust, spread, introduce in the air fryer and cook at 300 degrees F for 4 minutes.
5. Keep in the fridge for 4 hours before servin.

Strawberry Cream Cake

INGREDIENTS

- 2 cups all-purpose flour.
- 1/4 cup granulated sugar.
- 2 teaspoons baking powder.
- 1/4 teaspoon salt.
- 6 tablespoons butter, cold, cut into pieces.
- 1/2 cup fresh strawberries, chopped.
- 1/2 cup heavy cream, cold.
- 2 large eggs.
- 2 teaspoons vanilla extract.
- 1 teaspoon water.
- Granulated sugar, for topping.

Items needed: 1 round 2.5 inch cookie cutter

Servings: 12   25 minutes

DIRECTIONS

1. Sift together the flour, sugar, baking powder, and salt in a large bowl. Then cut the butter into the flour until the mixture resembles coarse crumbs.
2. Mix the strawberries into the flour mixture. Set aside.
3. In another bowl, whisk together the heavy cream, 1 egg, and the vanilla extract.
4. Fold the cream mixture into the flour mixture until combined, then roll it out to a 1½-inch thickness.
5. Use the 2.5-inch round cookie cutter to cut the scones.
6. Dip the scones in the mixture made from 1 egg and stirred water, Sprinkle with granulated sugar.
7. Line baking paper in the preheated air fryer basket. Then place the scones on top of paper.
8. Set time to 12 minutes in 330 °F.
9. Remove when golden brown and serve

Cranberry Cakes

Servings: 4   25 minutes

INGREDIENTS

- 1.5 cup milk.
- 2 cups All-purpose flour.
- 2 tbsp butter.
- 1/2 tsp baking powder.
- 1/2 tsp baking soda.
- 2 tsp vinegar.
- 2 tbsp sugar.
- 2 cups grated cranberries Muffin cups

DIRECTIONS

1. Mix well flour, sugar, butter, baking powder and grated cranberries together until to get acrumbly mixture.
2. Add the baking soda and the vinegar to the milk and mix continuously. Add this milk to the mixture in step 1 and create a batter, which you will need to transfer to the muffin cups.
3. Preheat the fryer to 330 F for 4 minutes. You will need to place the muffin cups in the basket and cover it. Bake the muffins for 15 minutes and check whether or not the muffins are cooked using a toothpick.
4. Remove the cups and serve hot.

Coffee Cheesecakes

Servings: 6   30 minutes

INGREDIENTS

The cheesecakes:
- 3 eggs.
- 2 tablespoons butter.
- 1/3 cup sugar.
- 8 ounces cream cheese.
- 3 tablespoons coffee.
- 1 tablespoon caramel syrup.

The frosting:
- 3 tablespoons butter.
- 2 tablespoons sugar.
- 3 tablespoons caramel syrup.
- 8 ounces mascarpone cheese, soft.

DIRECTIONS

1. Mix cream cheese with eggs, 2 tablespoons butter, coffee, 1 tablespoon caramel syrup and 1/3 cup sugar in your blender and pulse well.
2. Pour the above mixture into a cake pan that fits in your air fryer.
3. Introduce in the fryer and bake at 320 degrees F and bake for 20 minutes.
4. Leave aside to cool down and then put it in the fridge for 3 hours.
5. Meanwhile, mix 3 tablespoons butter with 3 tablespoons caramel syrup, 2 tablespoons sugar and mascarpone in a bowl, blend well, spoon this over cheesecakes and serve them.

Poppyseed Cake

INGREDIENTS

- 2 eggs, whisked.
- 3/4 cup sugar.
- 1.25 cups flour.
- 2 teaspoons lime zest, grated.
- 1 teaspoon baking powder.
- 1 tablespoon orange zest, grated.
- 1/2 cup butter, soft
- 1/2 teaspoon vanilla extract.
- 2 tablespoons poppy seeds.
- 1 cup milk.

For the cream:

- 1 cup sugar.
- 4 egg yolks.
- 3 tablespoons butter, melted.
- 1/2 cup passion fruit puree.

Servings: 6   40 minutes

DIRECTIONS

1. Mix flour with baking powder, 3/4 cup sugar, orange zest and lime zest in a bowl, and stir.
2. Add 1/2 cup butter, poppy seeds, eggs, vanilla and milk, stir using your mixer, pour into a cake pan that fits your air fryer and bake at 350 degrees F for about 30 minutes.
3. Meanwhile, heat up a pan with 3 tablespoons butter over medium heat, add sugar and stir until it dissolves. Add passion fruit puree and egg yolks gradually and whisk really well. Take off heat.
4. Take cake out of the fryer, cool it down a bit and cut into halves horizontally.
5. Spread 1/4 of passion fruit cream over one half, top with the other cake half and spread 1/4 of the cream on top.
6. Serve cold.

Lemon Pound Cake

INGREDIENTS

- 1 large egg.
- 1 cup all-purpose flour.
- 1 teaspoon baking powder.
- 1/4 teaspoon salt.
- 1 lemon, zested.
- 6 tablespoons unsalted butter, softened.
- 1/4 cup buttermilk.
- 1/4 cup granulated sugar.
- 1 tablespoon fresh lemon juice.

Items needed: 1 mini loaf pan, greased

Servings: 1 Mini Loaf   40 minutes

DIRECTIONS

1. Mix together the flour, baking powder, and salt in a bowl.
2. Beat the softened butter with an electric mixer for 3 minutes or until light and fluffy.
3. Add the sugar into the whipped butter, mix well in 1 minute.
4. Add the flour mixture into the butter mix well until fully incorporated.
5. Mix the egg, lemon juice, and lemon zest. Mix on low speed until fully incorporated. Pour in the buttermilk slowly while mixing at medium speed.
6. Add the batter to the greased mini loaf pan, filling all the way to the top.
7. Place cake into the preheated air fryer. Bake in 350 F on 35 minutes.
8. Take out and use immediately or serve cold.

Carrot Cake

Servings: 6   50 minutes

INGREDIENTS

- 1 egg
- 5 ounces flour.
- ½ teaspoon cinnamon powder
- ½ teaspoon baking soda
- ¾ teaspoon baking powder
- ½ teaspoon allspice
- ¼ cup pineapple juice
- ¼ teaspoon nutmeg, ground
- 1/3 cup carrots, grated
- 3 tablespoons yogurt
- ½ cup sugar
- 1/3 cup coconut flakes, shredded
- 4 tablespoons sunflower oil
- 1/3 cup pecans, toasted and chopped
- Cooking spray.

DIRECTIONS

1. Mix flour with baking soda and powder, salt, allspice, cinnamon and nutmeg in a bowl and stir.
2. In another bowl, mix egg with yogurt, sugar, pineapple juice, oil, carrots, pecans and coconut flakes and stir well.
3. Combine the two mixtures and stir well, pour this into a spring form pan that fits your air fryer which you've greased with cooking spray,
4. Put to your air fryer and bake on 320 degrees F for 40-45 minutes.
5. Leave cake to cool down, then cut and serve it.

Orange Cake

Servings: 12   40 minutes

INGREDIENTS

- 1 teaspoon baking powder.
- 6 eggs.
- 4 ounces yogur.
- 1 orange, peeled and cut into quarters.
- 1 teaspoon vanilla extract.
- 9 ounces flour.
- 2 ounces + 2 tablespoons sugar.
- 2 tablespoons orange zest.
- 4 ounces cream cheese.

DIRECTIONS

1. Puree oranges in a food processor.
2. Add flour, 2 tablespoons sugar, eggs, baking powder, vanilla extract and pulse well again.
3. Pour the above mixture into the baking pan. then put in an air fryer and bake at 330 degrees F for 16 minutes.
4. Meanwhile, mix cream cheese with orange zest, yogurt and the rest of the sugar in a bowl and stir well.
5. Place one cake layer on a plate, add half of the cream cheese mix, add the other cake layer and top with the rest of the cream cheese mix.
6. Spread it well, slice and serve.

Sponge Cake

Servings: 12   40 minutes

INGREDIENTS

- 1.5 cup milk.
- 1.7 cup sugar.
- 3 cups flour.
- 3 teaspoons baking powder.
- 1/2 cup cornstarch.
- 1 teaspoon baking soda.
- 1 cup olive oil.
- 1/4 cup lemon juice.
- 2 teaspoons vanilla extract.
- 2 cups water.

DIRECTIONS

1. Mix flour with cornstarch, baking powder, baking soda and sugar in a bowl and whisk well.
2. In second bowl, mix oil with milk, water, lemon juice and vanilla and whisk.
3. Combine the two mixtures, stir, pour in a greased baking dish that fits your air fryer.
4. Introduce in the fryer and bake at 350 degrees F for 20 minutes.
5. Leave cake to cool down, cut and serve.

Ricotta and Lemon Cake

Servings: 4   1 hour and 10 minutes

INGREDIENTS

- 8 eggs, whisked.
- 1/2 pound sugar.
- 3 pounds ricotta cheese.
- Zest from 1 orange.
- Zest from 1 lemon, grated.
- Grated Butter for the pan.

DIRECTIONS

1. Mix eggs with sugar, cheese, lemon and orange zest in a bowl, and stir very well.
2. Grease a baking pan that fits your air fryer with some batter, spread ricotta mixture.
3. Put in the fryer at 390 degrees F and bake for 30 minutes.
4. Reduce heat at 380 degrees F and bake for 40 more minutes.
5. Take out of the oven, leave cake to cool down and serve!

Tangerine Cake

Servings: 8   20 minutes

INGREDIENTS

- 1/2 cup milk.
- 3/4 cup sugar.
- 1/2 teaspoon vanilla extract.
- 2 cups flour.
- 1/4 cup olive oil.
- 1 teaspoon cider vinegar.
- Juice and zest from 1 tangerine.
- Juice and zest from 2 lemons.
- Tangerine segments, for serving.

DIRECTIONS

1. Mix flour with sugar in a bowl and stir.
2. In second bowl, mix oil with milk, vanilla extract, vinegar, lemon juice and zest and tangerine zest and whisk very well.
3. Combine the 2 mixtures in 2 bowls together, stir well, pour this into a cake pan that fits your air fryer, introduce in the fryer and cook at 360 degrees F for 20 minutes.
4. Serve right away with tangerine segments on top.

Strawberry Shortcakes

Servings: 6   45 minutes

INGREDIENTS

- 1 cup buttermilk.
- 1/3 cup butter.
- 1/4 cup+ 4 tablespoons sugar.
- 1.5 cup flour.
- 1 tablespoon mint, chopped.
- 1 teaspoon baking powder.
- 1/4 teaspoon baking soda.
- 1 egg, whisked.
- 2 cups strawberries, sliced.
- 1 tablespoon rum.
- 1 teaspoon lime zest, grated.
- 1/2 cup whipping cream.
- Cooking spray.

DIRECTIONS

1. Mix flour with 1/2 cup sugar, baking powder and baking soda in a bowl and stir.
2. In second bowl, mix buttermilk with egg, stir, add flour mixture in step 1 and whisk.
3. Scoop this dough into 6 jars greased with cooking spray, cover with tin foil, arrange them in your air fryer bake at 360 degrees F for 45 minutes.
4. Meanwhile, in third bowl, mix strawberries with 3 tablespoons sugar, rum, mint and lime zest, stir and leave aside in a cold place.
5. In another bowl, mix whipping cream with 1 tablespoon sugar and stir.
6. Take jars out, divide strawberry mix and whipped cream on top and serve.

Tomato Cake

Servings: 4   45 minutes

INGREDIENTS

- 1.5 cups flour.
- 1 teaspoon cinnamon powder.
- 1 teaspoon baking soda.
- 1 teaspoon baking
- 1 cup tomatoes chopped.
- 1/2 cup olive oil.
- powder.
- 3/4 cup maple syrup.
- 2 tablespoon apple cider vinega.

DIRECTIONS

1. Mix flour with baking powder, baking soda, cinnamon and maple syrup in a bowl, and stir well.
2. In second bowl, mix olive oil with tomatoes and vinegar and stir well.
3. Combine the 2 mixtures, stir well, pour into a greased round pan that fits your air fryer.
4. Introduce in the fryer and cook at 360 degrees F for 28-30 minutes.
5. Leave cake to cool down, slice and serve.

Black Tea Cake

Servings: 12   40 minutes

INGREDIENTS

- 6 tablespoons black tea powder.
- 2 cups milk.
- 1/2 cup butter.
- 2 cups sugar.
- 4 eggs.
- 2 teaspoons vanilla extract.
- 1/2 cup olive oil.
- 3.5 cups flour.
- 1 teaspoon baking soda.
- 3 teaspoons baking powder

For the cream:
- 6 tablespoons honey.
- 4 cups sugar.
- 1 cup butter, soft.

DIRECTIONS

1. Put the milk in a pot, heat up over low heat, add tea, stir well, take off heat and leave aside to cool down.
2. Mix 1/2 cup butter with 2 cups sugar, eggs, vegetable oil, vanilla extract, baking powder, baking soda and 3.5 cups flour in a bowl and stir everything really well.
3. Pour this mixture into 2 greased round pans, introduce each in the fryer at 330 degrees F and bake for 25 minutes.
4. Mix 1 cup butter with honey and 4 cups sugar in another bowl and stir really well.
5. Arrange one cake on a platter, spread the cream all over, top with the other cake and keep in the fridge until you serve it.

Plum Cake

Servings: 8   40 minutes

INGREDIENTS

- 1 egg, whisked.
- 7 ounces flour.
- 1 ounce butter, soft.
- 1 package dried yeast.
- 5 tablespoons sugar.
- 1.3 pounds plums, pitted and cut into quarters.
- 3 ounces warm milk.
- Zest from 1 lemon, grated
- 1 ounce almond flakes.

DIRECTIONS

1. Mix yeast with butter, flour and 3 tablespoons sugar in a bowl and stir well.
2. Add milk and egg and whisk for 4 minutes until your obtain a dough.
3. Arrange the dough in a spring form pan greased with some butter, put them your air fryer and which you've , cover and leave aside for 1 hour.
4. Arrange plumps on top of the butter, sprinkle the rest of the sugar, introduce in your air fryer at 350 degrees F, bake for 35 minutes.
5. Cool down, sprinkle almond flakes and lemon zest on top, slice and serve.

Chocolate Sponge Cake

Servings: 8   20 minutes

INGREDIENTS

- 1/2 cup condensed milk.
- 1 cup all-purpose flour.
- 1/2 cup cocoa powder.
- 1/2 tsp baking soda.
- 1/2 tsp baking powder.
- 1/2 cup oil.
- 3 tbsp powdered sugar,
- 1/2 cup soda.
- 1 tsp vanilla essence.
- Parchment or butter paper to line the tin

DIRECTIONS

1. Mix well the ingredients together to create a batter that is smooth and thick.
2. Grease the cake tin with butter and line the bottom with paper. Pour the mixture from step 1 into the cake tin and place it in the preheated air fryer basket.
3. Bake the cake for 15 minutes in 350 F and check whether or not the cake is cooked using a toothpick.
4. Remove the tin and cut the cake into slices and serve.

Maple Cupcakes

🍴 Servings: 4   🕐 30 minutes

INGREDIENTS

- 4 eggs.
- 4 tablespoons butter.
- 2 teaspoons cinnamon powder.
- 1/2 cup pure applesauce.
- 1/2 apple, cored and chopped.
- 1 teaspoon vanilla extract.
- 3/4 cup white flour.
- 4 teaspoons maple syrup.
- 1/2 teaspoon baking powder.

DIRECTIONS

1. Heat up a pan with the butter over medium heat, add applesauce, vanilla, eggs and maple syrup, stir, take off heat and leave aside to cool down.
2. Add flour, cinnamon, baking powder and apples, whisk.
3. Pour in a cupcake pan, introduce in your air fryer at 360 degrees F and bake for 20 minutes.
4. Leave cupcakes them to cool down, transfer to a platter and serve them.

Mini Chocolate Peanut Butter Cupcakes

INGREDIENTS

- 1 large egg.
- 1/2 cup whole milk.
- 1 cup sugar.
- 1 tsp baking powder.
- 1/4 cup vegetable oil.
- 1.5 tsp vanilla extract.
- 2/3 cup flour.
- 1/3 cup cocoa.
- 1/2 tsp baking soda.
- 1/2 tsp salt.
- 1 cup peanut butter.
- 1/4 cup water, boiling.
- Peanut Butter Frosting.
- 1 stick unsalted butter, softened.
- 2 cups confectioners sugar.
- 1 tbsp whole milk
- Garnish
- Chocolate pearls

Servings: 40   45 minutes

DIRECTIONS

1. Mix the egg, 1/2 cup milk, vegetable oil, and vanilla in a bowl and whisk to combine.
2. Combine the flour, sugar, cocoa, baking powder, baking soda, and salt with the egg mixture and stir.
3. Slowly add the boiling water to the mixture and whisk the mixture well.
4. Pour the batter into mini aluminum cupcake liners until about two-thirds of each cupcake liner is filled.
5. Place the cake pans in the preheated air fryer. Bake on 15-min in 350° F.
6. In that time, combine the peanut butter and the butter in a bowl. Add the confectioners' sugar and 1 tbsp. milk slowly until the frosting is creamy.
7. Let the cupcakes cool for 30 mins.
8. Top the cupcakes with the frosting and the chocolate pearls and serve.

Strawberry Cupcakes
With Creamy Strawberry Frosting

INGREDIENTS

- 100g Butter.
- 100g Caster Sugar.
- 2 Medium Eggs.
- 100g Self Raising Flour.
- 1/2 Tsp Vanilla Essence.
- 50g Butter.
- 100g Icing Sugar.
- 1/2 Tsp Pink Food Colouring.
- 1 Tbsp Whipped Cream.
- 1/4 Cup Fresh.
- Strawberries (blended)

Servings: 10   25 minutes

DIRECTIONS

1. Mix cream the butter and sugar in a large mixing bowl until the mixture is light and fluffy.
2. Add the vanilla essence and beat in the eggs one at a time. After adding each egg add a little of the flour. Gently fold in the rest of the flour.
3. Put them to little bun cases so that they are 1/3. Then put them in a preheated air fryer for 5 minutes and then bake for 8 minutes at 170 degrees Celsius.
4. While the cupcakes are cooking make the topping. Cream the butter and gradually add the icing sugar until you have a creamy mixture. Add the food colouring, whipped cream and blended strawberries and mix well
5. Once the cupcakes are cooked, using a piping bag add your topping to them doing circular motions so that you have that lovely cupcake look and serve.

Chocolate Souffle

INGREDIENTS

- 2 eggs, yolks separated from whites.
- Butter, for greasing Sugar, for coating.
- 2 tablespoons all-purpose flour.
- 3 ounces bittersweet chocolate, chopped.
- 1/4 cup unsalted butter.
- 3 tablespoons sugar.
- 1/2 teaspoon pure vanilla extract.
- Powdered sugar, for dusting.

Items needed : 2 (6-ounce) ramekins

Servings: 2   25 minutes

DIRECTIONS

1. Grease the ramekins with butter. Sprinkle sugar into the ramekins, shaking to spread around, then dumping out the excess.
2. Mix the chocolate and butter in a saucepan over medium heat, stirring until the chocolate is completely melted.
3. Whisk the egg yolks and vanilla extract. Then combine it the melted chocolate to prevent scrambling. Stir until there are no lumps and set aside to cool.
4. Beat the egg whites in another large bowl with an electric mixer at medium speed until they hold soft peaks. Then add the sugar to the egg whites, a little at a time, continuing to beat at medium speed. Once the sugar has been added, increase to high speed until the egg whites whites hold stiff peaks
5. Stir about 1/2 of the egg whites into the chocolate mixture to lighten it first. Then, add the chocolate mixture to the remaining whites, folding in gently but thoroughly.
6. Pour batter into the ramekins and place into the preheated air fryer. Bake in 330°F in 13-15 minutes.
7. Remove when done, dust the souffles with powdered sugar, and serve immediately.

Molten Chocolate Cakes

INGREDIENTS

Ganache:
- 1/4 cup heavy cream.
- 2 oz semi-sweet chocolate, chopped

Cakes:
- 5 tbsp unsalted butter, divided.
- 5 tbsp sugar, divided.
- 6 oz bittersweet or semi-sweet chocolate, chopped
- 1 pinch salt.
- 3 tbsp all-purpose flour.
- 2 large eggs, separated & divided.
- 1/2 tsp vanilla extract.
- Powdered sugar, for serving.
- Raspberries, for serving.
- Mint leaves, for serving.
- Vanilla ice cream, for serving
- Whipped cream, for serving.
- Whipped cream, for serving.

Servings: 2   25 minutes

DIRECTIONS

For the Ganache:
1. Place a saucepan on the stove top. Bring the cream to a simmer in the saucepan over low heat.
2. Place the chocolate in small bowl. Pour the cream over the chocolate, let sit for 2–3 mins, and then whisk to combine.
3. Chill the mixture until firm and then form it into six 1-in balls. Reserve the ganache in the refrigerator.

For the Cakes:
1. Pour 1 tsp sugar into each ramekin, turn to coat, and tap out any excess sugar.
2. Melt the chocolate and 4 tablespoons butter in a saucepan over medium heat and stir. Allow the chocolate to cool slightly and then stir in the egg yolks, vanilla, and flour.
3. Place the egg whites in the bowl of an electric mixer and whip until thickened and foamy. Add 3 tbsp sugar and continue beating just until stiff peaks form.
4. Fold the egg whites into the chocolate mixture until combined.
5. Evenly divide the batter in the prepared ramekins. Press a ganache ball into each ramekin and cover with batter.
6. Bake on 325° F in 15 mins until the top of the cakes are puffed and slightly firmed but not browned.
7. When done, remove the cakes and let rest for 3 mins. Top with powdered sugar, raspberries, and mint leaves. Serve with the vanilla ice cream and whipped cream.

Upside Down Pineapple Cake

🍴 Servings: 6   🕐 40 minutes

INGREDIENTS

- 2 tbsp butter (Preferably unsalted butter).
- 1/4 cup condensed milk.
- 2 tsp pineapple essence.
- 2 cups all purpose flour (split the flour into two parts – 1,5 cup and another 0.5 cup)
- 1/4 tsp baking powder.
- 1/4 tsp baking soda.
- Edible yellow food coloring.
- 1/2 cup drinking soda.
- 1/2 tbsp powdered sugar.

For the tin preparation:
- 6 slices pineapple.
- 3 tbsp sugar (This is to make the caramel)
- 8 cherries.

DIRECTIONS

1. Grease the tin with butter and line it on all sides with the butter paper. Sprinkle flour on tins. Add the slices of the pineapple to the base of the tin followed by the cherries. Cut the cherries into halves and place it on the cavities.
2. Melt the sugar and make it into a caramel. Pour this caramel into the tin and set it aside.
3. In a large bowl, sieve the flour, baking soda and powder. Add the butter to the bowl and beat the ingredients. Add the sugar and the condensed milk to the bowl and beat till you get auniform mixture. Add the essence and the yellow coloring followed by the dry ingredients to the bowl. Make sure that there are no lumps in the batter.
4. Pour the batter into the tin and put in the preheated air fryer for 5 minutes. Bake in 15 minutes, check whether or not the cake is cooked using a toothpick.
5. Remove the tin and cut the cake into slices and serve.

Sweet Potato Cheesecake

Servings: 4   15 minutes

INGREDIENTS

- 3/4 cup milk.
- 4 tablespoons butter, melted.
- 8 ounces cream cheese, soft.
- 6 ounces mascarpone, soft.
- 1 teaspoon vanilla extract.
- 2/3 cup graham crackers, crumbled.
- 1/4 teaspoons cinnamon powder.
- 2/3 cup sweet potato puree.

DIRECTIONS

1. Mix butter with crumbled crackers in a bowl, stir well, press on the bottom of a cake pan that fits your air fryer and keep in the fridge for now.
2. In second bowl, mix cream cheese with mascarpone, sweet potato, milk, puree, cinnamon and vanilla and whisk really well.
3. Take the pie crust out of the fridge, spread this over crust, introduce in your air fryer, cook at 300 degrees F for 5 minutes.
4. Keep in the fridge for a few hours before serving.

Cardamom Cakes

🍴 Servings: 4   🕐 15 minutes

INGREDIENTS

- 2 cups All-purpose flour.
- 1.5 cup milk.
- 1 tbsp cardamom powder.
- 1/2 tsp baking powder.
- 1/2 tsp baking soda.
- 2 tbsp butter.
- 2 tbsp sugar.
- Muffin cups.

DIRECTIONS

1. In a bowl, mix the dry ingredients well to get a acrumbly mixture.
2. In another bowl, mix well the baking soda and the vinegar to the milk, add this milk to the mixture in step 1 and create a batter. Pour into the muffin cups.
3. Preheat the fryer to 300 F for 4 minutes. Put the muffin cups in the basket and bake for 15 minutes.
4. Remove the cups and serve hot.

Stuffed French Toast

Servings: 1   15 minutes

INGREDIENTS

- 2 eggs.
- 1 Slice brioche bread, 2.5 inches thick, preferably stale.
- 4 ounces cream cheese.
- 1 teaspoon cinnamon.
- 2 tablespoons milk.
- 2 tablespoons heavy cream.
- 3 tablespoons sugar.
- 1/2 teaspoon vanilla extract.
- Pistachios, chopped, for topping.
- Maple syrup, for serving.
- Cooking spray.

DIRECTIONS

1. Cut a slit in the middle of the brioche slice, stuff the inside of the slit with cream cheese. Set aside.
2. Whisk together the eggs, milk, heavy cream, sugar, cinnamon, and vanilla extract in a bowl.
3. Soak the stuffed French toast in the egg mixture for 10 seconds on each side. Then Spray each side of the French toast with cooking spray.
4. Place the French toast into the preheated air fryer. Bake in 10 minutes on 350°F.
5. Remove the French toast carefully when done cooking.
6. Top with chopped pistachios and serve with maple syrup.

Crunchy French Toast

Servings: 1   15 minutes

INGREDIENTS

Egg Mixture:
- 1 large egg.
- 1/4 cup heavy cream.
- 1 tsp vanilla.
- 1 ripe banana, mashed.
- 1/4 tsp salt.
- 1 tbsp unsalted butter, melted.
- 1 brioche loaf, cut into 12 slices.
- 1 cup cinnamon crunch cereal, crushed finely.

Topping:
- 1/2 pecans, chopped
- 1/2 cup dried cranberries
- 1 ripe banana, sliced.
- For Serving: maple syrup

DIRECTIONS

1. In a bowl, mix well the egg, vanilla, salt, butter, cream, and the mashed banana.
2. Dip the brioche slices into the egg mixture in step 1 and coat the bread with the cereal crumbs.
3. Spray the Air Flow Racks with nonstick spray. Put the French toast on the Basket. Bake at 400° F for 10 mins. Flip the French toast halfway through the cooking time for ripen evenly.
4. Top with the pecans, dried cranberries, syrup, and slices of the other banana.

Simple Pancakes

Servings: 14   15 minutes

INGREDIENTS

- 120g Pancake Mix of your choice.
- 60g Whey/Casein Blend Vanilla Protein Powder.
- 30g PB Party Protein Cookie Butter Powder.
- 24g Coconut Flour.
- 8g Zero Cal Sweetener of your choice.
- 8g Baking Powder.
- 150g Egg Whites.
- Unsweetened Vanilla.
- Almond Milk to the consistency of batter

DIRECTIONS

1. Mix all of your dry ingredients in a bowl to avoid clumping, then add in your wet ingredients and mix some more. Add in a little bit of almond milk at a time and mix, then repeat until you reach a batter-like consistency.
2. Add 1/14th of your batter to the pan. Place a cover on top and cook your pancakes until you see little air bubbles coming from the top of the pancakes, then flip them over.
3. Bake the pancakes on that side for another 2 minutes and repeat this process until all 14 pancakes are cooked.

TIP: If you want to store it in the fridge, Once they're cool, put them in a Ziplock bag and suck all the air out of the bag , then put them in your freezer. To reheat them, use either your toaster or air fryer!

Honey and Orange Pancakes

Servings: 16 18 minutes

INGREDIENTS

- 3 eggs.
- 1 orange (zested).
- 3 tbsp Butter.
- 1.5 cups almond flour.
- 2 tsp dried parsley.
- 1 tbsp honey.
- 2 tsp dried basil.
- Salt and Pepper to taste.

DIRECTIONS

1. Mix well the ingredients together in a bowl until the mixture is smooth and well balanced.
2. Take a pancake mold and grease it with butter. Add the batter to the mold and place it in preheated air fryer basket. Bake in 320 F for 5 mins or till both the sides of the pancake have browned on both sides and serve with maple syrup.

Zucchini Pancakes

Servings: 12   20 minutes

INGREDIENTS

- 3 eggs.
- 2 zucchinis (shredded).
- 2 tsp dried parsley.
- 1.5 cups almond flour.
- 3 tbsp Butter
- 2 tsp dried basil.
- Salt and Pepper to taste.

DIRECTIONS

1. Mix well the ingredients together in a bowl until the mixture is smooth and well balanced.
2. Take a pancake mold and grease it with butter. Add the batter to the mold and place it in preheated air fryer basket. Bake in 320 F for 5 mins or till both the sides of the pancake have browned on both sides and serve with maple syrup.

Pumpkin Pancakes

Servings: 12   15 minutes

INGREDIENTS

- 3 eggs.
- 1 large pumpkin (shredded).
- 2 tsp dried basil.
- 1.5 cups almond flour.
- 2 tsp dried parsley.
- Salt and Pepper to taste.
- 3 tbsp Butter.

DIRECTIONS

1. Mix well the ingredients together in a bowl until the mixture is smooth and well balanced.
2. Take a pancake mold and grease it with butter. Add the batter to the mold and place it in preheated air fryer basket. Bake in 320 F for 5 mins or till both the sides of the pancake have browned on both sides and serve with maple syrup.

Grilled Cheese

Servings: 2   15 minutes

INGREDIENTS

- 4 slices white bread.
- 3 tablespoons butter, melted.
- 1/2 cup sharp cheddar
- Cheese, shredded, divided

DIRECTIONS

1. Brush butter on each side of the bread slices.
2. Split the cheese evenly between 2 slices of bread and top with remaining bread slices to make 2 sandwiches.
3. Place the sandwiches into the preheated air fryer. Bake at 320°F for 5 minutes.
4. Cut diagonally and serve.

Triple Berry Turnovers

INGREDIENTS

- 1/2 cup mixed berries, chopped.
- 1/2 cup berry jam.
- 1 pkg (14 oz) refrigerator rolled pie pastry.
- 1 egg.
- 1/2 cup icing sugar.
- 1 tbsp milk.

Servings: 6   40 minutes

DIRECTIONS

1. Mix together berries and jam. Let stand for 8 minutes.
2. On lightly floured surface, roll out pie pastry; using 5-inch ring mold or round cookie cutter, cut out 6 rounds.
3. Whisk egg with 2 tsp water; brush over one-half of the edges of pastry rounds. Spread 1 tbsp berry jam over egg-washed half of pastry rounds, leaving border; fold remaining pastry over jam and press edges firmly with fork to seal. Pierce top of tarts with fork to make steam vents. Warm up remaining berry jam.
4. Brush top of tarts with remaining egg wash. Place tarts in bowl of air-fryer. Bake at 300 F in 12 - 15 minutes or until golden and flaky. Let cool completely.
5. Stir icing sugar with milk until smooth. Drizzle turnovers with icing and top with remaining berry jam.

Tip: Try peaches and peach jam, apples and apple butter or cherries and cherry jam.

Mushroom Cakes

Servings: 8   20 minutes

INGREDIENTS

- 4 ounces mushrooms, chopped.
- 14 ounces milk
- 1 yellow onion, chopped.
- 1 tablespoon butter.
- ½ teaspoon nutmeg, ground.
- 1.5 tablespoon flour.
- 2 tablespoons olive oil.
- 1 tablespoon bread crumbs
- Salt and black pepper to the taste.

DIRECTIONS

1. Heat up a pan with the butter over medium heat, add mushrooms and onion, stir, cook for 3 minutes, add flour, stir well again and take off heat.
2. Add milk slowly to the above mixture, then add salt, pepper and nutmeg, stir and leave aside to cool down completely.
3. Mix oil with bread crumbs and whisk in a bowl.
4. Take spoonfuls of the mushroom filling, add to breadcrumbs mix, coat well, shape patties out of this mix, place them in your air fryer's basket and cook at 380 degrees F for 10 minutes.
5. Take out the cake, wait for it to cool down and enjoy.

Cauliflower Cakes

Servings: 6   20 minutes

INGREDIENTS

- 3.5 cups cauliflower rice.
- 1/4 cup white flour.
- 2 eggs.
- Cooking spray
- 1/2 cup parmesan, grated. Salt and black pepper to the taste.

DIRECTIONS

1. Mix cauliflower rice with salt and pepper in a bowl, stir and squeeze excess water.
2. Transfer cauliflower to other bowl, add eggs, pepper, salt, flour and parmesan, stir really well and shape your cakes.
3. Grease air fryer with cooking spray, heat it up at 400 degrees, add cauliflower cakes and cook them for 10 minutes flipping them halfway.
4. Divide cauliflower cakes on plates and serve.

MUFFIN

Egg Muffins

Servings: 4   25 minutes

INGREDIENTS

- 1 egg
- 3.5 ounces white flour
- 2 tablespoons olive oil
- 2 ounces parmesan, grated
- 3 tablespoons milk
- 1 tablespoon baking powder
- A splash of Worcestershire sauce

DIRECTIONS

1. Mix eggs with flour, oil, baking powder, milk, Worcestershire and parmesan cheese in a bowl whisk well and divide into 4 silicon muffin cups.
2. Arrange cups in your air fryer's cooking basket, cover and bake at 392, degrees F for 15 minutes.
3. Serve warm for breakfast.

Cheese Corn Muffins

Servings: 6   30 minutes

INGREDIENTS

- 60 gram all-purpose flour.
- 79 gram corn flour.
- 38 gram white sugar.
- 6 gram salt.
- 7 gram baking powder (baking soda)
- 120 ml of fresh milk.
- 45 gr butter, melted.
- 1 egg.
- 165 grams of corn.
- 3 sprigs of scallions, chopped
- 120 gr cheddar cheese, finely grated.
- Cooking spray.

DIRECTIONS

1. Mix flour, cornstarch, sugar, salt and baking powder in a large bowl.
2. In another bowl, whisk together the milk, butter, and eggs. Gently mix the dry mixture into the bowl of the wet mixture. Gently toss corn, scallions, and grated cheddar cheese.
3. Heat the air fryer at 160 degrees for 3 minutes.
4. Spray cooking oil on muffin molds to prevent sticking and pour in flour no more than 3/4. Place the muffin pan in the preheated frying basket and bake on 320 degrees F for 15 minutes.
5. Enjoy the Muffins with butter or eat it right away.

Blueberry Muffins

Servings: 6   45 minutes

INGREDIENTS

- 275g Egg Whites.
- 75g Whey/Casein Blend Vanilla Protein Powder.
- 100g Frozen Blueberries
- 30g Blueberry Pastry Protein Cookie Butter Powder.
- 30g All Purpose Flour.
- 10g Baking Powder.
- 20g Coconut Flour.
- 10g Zero Cal Sweetener of your choice.
- 275g Plain Nonfat Greek Yogurt.
- 100g Unsweetened Apple Sauce.

DIRECTIONS

1. Mix well all the dry ingredients together in a bowl to avoid clumping, then add in your wet ingredients and mix some more. Don't any chunks or clumps. When everything's mixed together, let the batter sit for 15-20 minutes to thicken up.
2. Mix frozen blueberries with the batter, then spray silicon jump muffin molds with nonstick cooking spray. Evenly pour the batter into 6 molds. Be sure to leave enough space between them get don't oddly shaped muffins.
3. Baking the muffins at 250 degrees F for 32-35 minutes. When done, let them cool in their molds for 10-15 minutes, then serve.

Pumpkin Muffins

Servings: 18   25 minutes

INGREDIENTS

- 1/4 cup butter.
- 1/2 teaspoon baking powder.
- 1/4 cup flour.
- 1/2 cup sugar.
- 3/4 cup pumpkin puree.
- 1 teaspoon cinnamon powder.
- 2 tablespoons flaxseed meal.
- 1/2 teaspoon nutmeg, ground.
- 1 egg.
- 1/2 teaspoon baking soda.

DIRECTIONS

1. Mix butter with pumpkin puree and egg in a bowl, and blend well.
2. Add flaxseed meal, sugar, flour, baking powder, baking soda, nutmeg and cinnamon and stir well.
3. Use a spoon to scoop the mixture into the muffin cups. Then put them in your air fryer at 350 degrees F and bake for 15 minutes.
4. Serve muffins cold as a snack.

Coffee Streusel Muffins

🍴 Servings: 6   🕒 18 minutes

INGREDIENTS

Muffins:
- 1 egg.
- 3/4 cup all-purpose flour.
- 1/2 teaspoon cinnamon.
- 1/4 cup light brown sugar.
- 1/2 teaspoon baking soda.
- 1 teaspoon baking powder.
- 1/2 cup sour cream.
- 1/2 teaspoon salt.
- 3 tablespoons unsalted butter, melted.
- 1 teaspoon vanilla.
- Cooking spray

Items meeded: 1 (6-cup) muffin pan or baking cups.

Crumb Topping:
- 3 tablespoons all-purpose flour.
- 1/4 teaspoon cinnamon.
- 1 tablespoon white sugar.
- 1.5 tablespoons light brown sugar.
- 1 tablespoon unsalted butter, melted.
- 1/4 teaspoon salt.

DIRECTIONS

1. Mix all the crumb topping ingredients together in a bowl until they form coarse crumbs.
2. Combine the muffins' flour, light brown sugar, baking powder, baking soda, cinnamon, and salt in another bowl.
3. Whisk the egg, sour cream, butter, and vanilla extract together in a separate bowl until well combined.
4. Mix well the wet ingredients into the dry. Grease muffin cups with cooking spray and pour batter in until cups are ¾ full.
5. Sprinkle the top of the muffins with the crumb topping. Put the muffins into the preheated air fryer, bake to 350°F in 12 minutes.
6. Take the muffin out and serve hot or cold.

Oats Muffins

INGREDIENTS

- 2 cups All-purpose flour.
- 1.5 cup milk.
- 1/2 tsp baking powder.
- 1/2 tsp baking soda
- 2 tbsp butter.
- 1 cup sugar.
- 3 tsp vinegar.
- 1 cup oats.
- 1/2 tsp vanilla essence.
- Muffin cups or butter paper cups.

Servings: 6   18 minutes

DIRECTIONS

1. Mix the dry ingredients together to get a acrumbly mixture.
2. Divide the milk into two equal parts, then add one to the baking soda and the other to the vinegar.
3. Mix both milk mixtures together and wait until the milk starts to foam. Add this mixture to the crumb mixture and start whisking the ingredients at a high speed.
4. Once you have a smooth batter, pour the mixture into the muffin cups. Preheat the fryer to 300 degrees F for 5 minutes. Then place the muffin cups in the basket and bake at 320 degrees F for 15 minutes Remove and serve hot.

Blueberry Lemon Muffins

INGREDIENTS

- 1 cup all-purpose flour.
- 1/2 teaspoon lemon juice.
- 1/4 teaspoon baking soda.
- 1/2 cup coconut milk or soy milk.
- 1 lemon, zested.
- 1 teaspoon baking powder.
- 1/4 cup granulated sugar.
- 1/4 teaspoon salt.
- 1 cup fresh blueberries.
- 3 tablespoons liquidated coconut oil.
- 1/2 teaspoon vanilla extract.
- Cooking spray.

Items needed: 1 (6-cup) muffin pan or baking cups.

Servings: 8   25 minutes

DIRECTIONS

1. Mix lemon juice and coconut/soy milk in a small bowl, then set aside. Mix together flour, baking powder, baking soda, and salt in a separate bowl.
2. Blend sugar, coconut oil, lemon zest, and vanilla extract in third bowl. Combine with lemon-milk mixture in step 1 and stir.
3. Mix the dry mixture into the wet gradually, until smooth. Gently fold in blueberries.
4. Grease muffin cups with cooking spray and pour in batter until cups are ¾ full. Put the muffins carefully into the preheated air fryer. Bake for 300°F in 15 minutes.
5. Remove muffins when done cooking, let cool then serve.

Orange Cranberry Muffins

INGREDIENTS

- 1 egg.
- 1/4 cup sugar.
- 1 cup all-purpose flour.
- 1/4 teaspoon salt.
- 1 cup cranberries.
- 1 teaspoon baking powder.
- 1/4 teaspoon baking soda.
- 1/4 cup orange juice.
- 1/4 cup vegetable oil.
- 1 orange, zested.
- Cooking spray.
- 1 (6-cup) muffin pan or baking cups

Servings: 6   25 minutes

DIRECTIONS

1. In a large bowl, mix well the flour, sugar, baking powder, baking soda, salt, and cranberries.
2. In second bowl, whisk the egg, orange juice, vegetable oil, and orange zest. Then mix the wet ingredients with the dry ingredients until combined.
3. Grease the muffin cups with cooking spray and pour in batter until cups are 3/4 full. Put the muffins carefully into the preheated air fryer. Bake muffin for 300°F in 15 minutes.
4. Take out, let cool and serve.

Chocolate Chip Muffins

INGREDIENTS

- 1 cup all-purpose flour
- 1/4 cup granulated sugar.
- 1/2 teaspoon vanilla extract.
- 1/2 cup coconut milk or soy milk.
- 3 tablespoons liquidated coconut oil.
- 1/4 teaspoon salt
- 1 teaspoon baking powder
- 2 tablespoons cocoa powder
- 1/4 teaspoon baking soda
- 1/2 cup dark chocolate chips
- 1/4 cup pistachios, cracked (optional)
- Cooking spray
- Muffin pan or baking cups

Servings: 8   25 minutes

DIRECTIONS

1. In a bowl, mix sugar, coconut/soy milk, coconut oil, and vanilla extractthen set aside.
2. In a second bowl, mix together flour, cocoa powder, baking powder, baking soda, and salt.
3. Mix the dry ingredients into the wet ingredients gradually, until smooth. Then fold in chocolate chips and pistachios.
4. Preheat the Air Fryer for 300°F in 4 mins.
5. Grease muffin cups with cooking spray and pour in batter until cups are 3/4 full.
6. Put the muffins into the preheated air fryer. Bake muffin for 300°F in 15 minutes. Then take out, let cool and serve.

Chocolate Espresso Muffins

INGREDIENTS

- 1 large egg
- 1 cup all-purpose flour
- 3/4 cup light brown sugar
- 3/4 cup milk
- 1/2 cup cocoa powder
- 1/2 teaspoon baking soda
- 1/2 teaspoon baking powder
- 1/2 teaspoon instant espresso powder
- 1/4 teaspoon salt
- 1/2 cup vegetable oil
- 1 teaspoon vanilla extract
- 1 teaspoon apple cider vinegar
- Cooking spray
- Muffin pan or baking cups.

Servings: 8   25 minutes

DIRECTIONS

1. In a large bowl, mix the flour, cocoa powder, light brown sugar, baking powder, espresso powder, baking soda, and salt.
2. In second bowl, whisk the egg, milk, vanilla extract, apple cider vinegar, and vegetable oil.
3. Mix the wet ingredients with the dry until combined.
4. Grease the muffin cups with cooking spray and pour in batter until cups are 3/4 full. Put the muffins into the preheated air fryer. Bake muffin for 300°F in 15 minutes.
5. Then take out, let cool and serve.

Banana Nut Muffins

INGREDIENTS

- 200g Egg Whites
- 400g Banana
- 12g Baking Powder
- 100g Unsweetened Vanilla Almond Milk
- 30g Crushed Walnuts
- 45g Coconut Flour
- 90g PEScience Gourmet Vanilla Select Protein
- 45g PB Party Protein Cookie Butter Powder
- 12g Zero Cal Sweetener of your Choice
- 5g Ground Cinnamon

Servings: 6   40 minutes

DIRECTIONS

1. In a large bowl, mash your banana until there aren't any chunks, then mix in your egg whites.
2. Mix your dry ingredients together in another, then combine the dry ingredients with the wet.
3. Spray your muffin tins with nonstick cooking spray and evenly add your batter to each. Add your muffins to the air fryer for 30 minutes at 250 degrees F until the tops start cracking and you see some golden-brown spots.
4. Take the muffins out of your air fryer, let them cool, then enjoy.

Note: *If want to lower the calories and fats a good bit, just take out the walnuts!*

Banana Muffins

Servings: 8   15 minutes

INGREDIENTS

- 1 banana, peeled and sliced into 16 pieces.
- 16 baking cups crust.
- 1 tablespoon vegetable oil.
- 3/4 cup chocolate chips.
- 1/4 cup peanut butter.

DIRECTIONS

1. Put chocolate chips in a small pot, heat over low heat, stir until the chocolate melts, and then turn off the heat.
2. Mix peanut butter with coconut oil in a bowl, and whisk well.
3. Firt, spoon 1 teaspoon chocolate mix in a cup, then add 1 banana slice and top with 1 teaspoon butter mix in step 2.
4. Repeat with the remaining cups, put them all in a dish that will fit your air fryer, cook at 320 degrees F for 5 minutes, then move to a freezer and keep there until you're ready to serve them as a snack.

Cheesy Cornbread Muffins

Servings: 6   25 minutes

INGREDIENTS

- 1 egg
- 1/2 cup all-purpose flour.
- 1 cup corn
- 1/2 cup cornmeal
- 1/2 cup milk
- 3 tablespoons white sugar
- 1 teaspoon salt
- 1.5 teaspoons baking powder
- 3 tablespoons butter, melted
- 3 scallions, chopped
- 3 ounces cheddar cheese, grated
- Cooking spray
- Muffin pan or baking cups

DIRECTIONS

1. In a bowl, mix flour, cornmeal, sugar, salt, and baking powder.
2. Whisk together milk, butter, and egg until well combined.
3. Combine dry ingredients with wet ingredients. Fold in corn, scallions, and cheddar cheese.
4. Grease muffin cups with cooking spray and pour in batter until cups are 3/4 full. Put the muffins into the preheated air fryer. Bake muffin for 300°F in 15 minutes.
5. Then take out, let cool and serve.

Chocolate Muffins

Servings: 12   25 minutes

INGREDIENTS

- 2 Medium Eggs
- 100g Butter
- 200g Self Raising
- 225 Caster Sugar
- 1/2 Tsp Vanilla Essence
- 25g Cocoa Powder
- 75g Milk Chocolate
- 5 Tbsp Milk Water

DIRECTIONS

1. Mix the flour, sugar and cocoa in a large mixing bowl. Rub in the butter until have a breadcrumbs consistency.
2. In second bowl, crack the eggs, add the milk and mix well. Add the egg/milk mixture into the large mixing bowl and mix well.
3. Add the vanilla essence, mix well and then add a little water if it is too thick. You have something that resembles a bun mix.
4. Using a rolling pin bash your milk chocolate in a sandwich bag until they are a mix of sizes. Add it to the bowl and mix again for the last time.
5. Spoon into little bun cases and put the muffins into the preheated air fryer. Bake for 9 minutes on 180c followed by 6 minutes on 160c. And serve.

DONUTS

Simple Donuts

Servings: 6   25 minutes

INGREDIENTS

- 4 tablespoons butter, soft.
- 1/2 cup sour cream.
- 1.5 teaspoon baking powder.
- 2 egg yolks.
- 2.25 cups white flour.
- 1 teaspoon cinnamon powder.
- 1/2 cup sugar.
- 1/3 cup caster sugar.

DIRECTIONS

1. Mix 2 tablespoons of butter with simple sugar and egg yolks and beat well in a bowl.
2. Add half of the sour cream to the bowl and stir.
3. In another bowls, mix flour with baking powder, stir. Then add the egg mixture in step 1 and 2 and stir well
4. Stir until you obtain a dough, transfer it to a floured working surface, roll it out and cut big circles with smaller ones in the middle.
5. Brush doughnuts with the rest of the butter, heat up your air fryer at 360 degrees F in 3 minutes, place doughnuts inside and bake them for 8 minutes.
6. Mix cinnamon with caster sugar in a bowl.
7. Arrange doughnuts on plates and dip them in cinnamon sugar mixture before serving.

Strawberry Donuts

Servings: 4   25 minutes

INGREDIENTS

- 8 ounces flour.
- 1 tablespoon brown sugar.
- 1 tablespoon white sugar.
- 1 egg.
- 2.5 tablespoons butter.
- 4 ounces whole milk.
- 1 teaspoon baking powder.

For the strawberry icing:
- 2 tablespoons butter.
- 3.5 ounces icing sugar.
- ½ teaspoon pink coloring.
- ¼ cup strawberries, chopped.
- 1 tablespoon whipped cream.

DIRECTIONS

1. Mix butter, 1 tablespoon brown sugar, 1 tablespoon white sugar and flour in a bowl and stir.
2. In another bowl, mix egg with 1.5 tablespoons butter and milk and stir well.
3. Combine the 2 mixtures, stir, shape donuts from this mix, place them in your air fryer's basket and bake at 360 degrees F for 15-18 minutes.
4. Put 1 tablespoon butter, icing sugar, food coloring, whipped cream and strawberry puree and whisk well.
5. Arrange donuts on a platter and pour the strawberry sauce on top and enjoy.

Everything Bagels

Servings: 6   15 minutes

INGREDIENTS

- 50g Egg Whites
- 45g All Purpose Flour
- 3g Baking Powder
- 8g Coconut Flour
- 3g Everything Bagel Seasoning
- 100g Plain Nonfat Greek Yogurt

DIRECTIONS

1. In a bowl, mix all of your dry ingredients together, then add in your wet ingredients and mix everything together.
2. Spray mini silicone bagel molds with nonstick cooking spray and evenly spread your batter to each.
3. Air fry the bagels at 360 degrees F for 8 minutes, then open the air fryer, flip the other side of the bagel, bake for another 4-6 minutes until golden.
4. When they're done, let the bagels cool on a cooling rack. Don't cut them out right away as they will be super soft in the middle.

Oreo Mini Donuts

Servings: 27   25 minutes

INGREDIENTS

- 412g Egg Whites
- 75g Whey/Casein Blend Vanilla Protein Powder
- 30g Black Cocoa Powder
- 75g All Purpose Flour
- 36g Brownie Batter Protein Cookie Butter Powder
- 412g Plain Nonfat Greek Yogurt
- 15g Zero Cal Sweetener of your choice
- 15g Baking Powder
- 150g Unsweetened Apple Sauce.

DIRECTIONS

1. Add all your dry ingredients into a bowl and mix well to avoid clumping. Then add your wet ingredients and mix until combined.
2. Add mini donut silicone molds to your air fryer and spray with non stick cooking spray.
3. Add your batter to each leaving a little bit from the top because these will rise. Bake for 250 degrees F in 15 minutes, then open the air fryer, flip the other side of the bagel, bake for 5 more minutes at the same temperature.
4. Then add whatever frosting your heart desires on top along with toppings and enjoy!

Vanilla Mini Donuts

Servings: 27   25 minutes

INGREDIENTS

- 412g Egg Whites
- 75g All Purpose Flour
- 75g Whey/Casein Blend Vanilla Protein Powder
- 15g Baking Powder
- 36g Birthday Cake Batter Protein Cookie Butter Powder
- 30g Coconut Flour
- 15g Zero Cal Sweetener of your choice
- 412g Plain Nonfat Greek Yogurt
- 150g Unsweetened Apple Sauce

DIRECTIONS

1. Add all your dry ingredients into a bowl and mix well to avoid clumping. Then add your wet ingredients and mix until combined.
2. Add mini donut silicone molds to your air fryer and spray with non stick cooking spray.
3. Add your batter to each leaving a little bit from the top because these will rise. Bake for 250 degrees F in 15 minutes, then open the air fryer, flip the other side of the bagel, bake for 5 more minutes at the same temperature.
4. Then add whatever frosting your heart desires on top along with toppings and enjoy!

Cinnamon Sugar Donuts

INGREDIENTS

- 250 ml Lukewarm milk.
- 3.5 tsp Instant dry yeast.
- 1 pc Egg, beaten, room temperature.
- 450 grams All purpose flour, plus extra for dusting.
- 1 tbsp Shallot choppe.
- 55 grams Caster sugar.
- 1/4 tsp Salt.
- 30 grams Unsalted butter, melted.

The cinnamon sugar coating:
- 3/4 cup White sugar.
- A pinch Salt.
- 1.5 tsp Cinnamon powder.

DIRECTIONS

🍴 10 Donuts   🕐 30 minutes

1. Whisk the yeast and milk together in a bowl. Add 1 tsp of the flour and 1 tsp of the sugar. Whisk until combined. Let sit for 10-15 minutes.
2. Place the remaining flour, remaining sugar, and salt in a bowl. Mix with a hand or mixer.
3. Add egg while mixing. Next, add melted butter and yeast mixture. Knead until dough is smooth and elastic.
4. With hands scrape the dough into a lightly oiled bowl. Cover and set aside to rest for 1–1 1/2 hours, or until the dough has doubled in size.
5. Line with baking paper the Air Fryer tray.
6. Generously flour a surface and gently tip the dough out onto it. Using a floured rolling pin, gently roll the dough out to a 1 cm (1/2 inch) thickness.
7. Using a floured 8 cm (3 1/4 inch) round cookie cutter, cut out 10 rounds from the dough, making sure you cut them as close together as possible. Use a floured 3 cm (1 1/4 inch) round cookie cutter to cut out holes from the center of each larger circle. Carefully transfer the donuts and their holes to the prepared trays, spreading them out in a single layer. Cover with kitchen towels then allow to rest for 40 minutes at room temperature, or until the donuts have doubled in size.Preheat Instant Air Fryer to 180oC in 12 minutes.
8. Add the tray in the Air Fryer and turn the donuts on the other side halfway through cooking time.
9. Remove from Air Fryer and allow to cool for 3 minutes.
10. Combine cinnamon-sugar ingredients in a deep bowl
11. Brush the donuts with melted butter and toss in the bowl of cinnamon-sugar.

COOKIES

Macaroons

Servings: 20   18 minutes

INGREDIENTS

- 4 egg whites.
- 2 tablespoons sugar.
- 2 cup coconut, shredded.
- 1 teaspoon vanilla extract.

DIRECTIONS

1. Mix egg whites with stevia and beat using your mixer then pour them into the bowl.
2. Add coconut and vanilla extract, whisk again, shape small balls out of this mix, introduce them in your air fryer and cook at 340 degrees F for 8-10 minutes.
3. Let the macaroons cool completely and serve.

Coconut Macaroons

Servings: 6   25 minutes

INGREDIENTS

- 1 egg white
- 1/4 teaspoon salt
- 1/4 cup sweetened condensed milk
- 1/4 teaspoon vanilla extract
- 1/4 teaspoon almond extract
- 1.7 cups shredded, unsweetened coconut, divided

DIRECTIONS

1. In a bowl, mix condensed milk, egg white, almond extract, vanilla extract, and salt.
2. Add 1.5 cups shredded coconut and mix until well combined- Mixture should be able to hold its shape.
3. Form 1.5-inch balls with your hands. On another plate, add 1/4 cup shredded coconut. Roll the macaroons in the shredded coconut until covered.
4. Put the coconut macaroons to the preheated air fryer. Bake for 300°F in 15 minutes
5. Remove when done, let macaroons cool, then serve.

Honey and Oats Cookie

Servings: 18   25 minutes

INGREDIENTS

- 1 cups flour
- 1 cup all-purpose flour
- 1/2 cup milk
- 1 tsp baking powder
- 1 tbsp liquid glucose
- 2 tbsp powdered sugar
- 1/2 cup oats
- 1 tbsp unsalted butter
- 2 tsp honey

DIRECTIONS

1. In a bowl, mix the dry ingredients together and warm the glucose with a little water. Mix the glucose, honey and the butter to the bowl followed by the milk.
2. Roll the dough using a pin. Create cookies and set them on a prepared baking tray.
3. Preheat the fryer to 300 Fahrenheit for 4 minutes. Then put the baking tray in the basket and bake to 250 Fahrenheit in 15 minutes. Turn the cookies in the tray to ensure that they are cooked uniformly.
4. When the cookies have cooled, store them in an airtight container and serve

Danisa Cookie

🍴 Servings: 18   🕐 25 minutes

INGREDIENTS

- 120 gr all-purpose flour.
- 90 gr Unsalted Butter.
- 1 Egg white.
- 50 gr Powdered sugar. (or fine granulated sugar)
- Raisins

DIRECTIONS

1. Put unsalted butter in a bowl, mash it and then add the egg whites and stir well before adding powdered sugar. Beat the flour mixture until the sugar is completely dissolved.
2. Sift the prepared flour into the flour mixture, then continue to mix until the dough is smooth.
3. Spread baking paper (or foil) on the grid of the air fryer. Then, you scoop the flour mixture into the ice cream catcher. Shape the cookies to your liking.
4. Bake the cake at 140 degrees Celsius for 12 minutes, then flip the other side of the cake and continue to bake at 160 degrees Celsius for another 5 minutes to complete.

Cookie Custards

Servings: 6   25 minutes

INGREDIENTS

- 2 tbsp margarine.
- 1 cup all-purpose flour
- 1/2 cup custard powder
- 1/2 cup icing sugar
- A pinch of baking soda and baking powder

DIRECTIONS

1. Mix cream the margarine and sugar together. Then add the remaining ingredients and fold them together.
2. Prepare a baking tray greased with butter. Roll the dough into balls, roll the balls in the flour and place in the baking tray. Preheat the fryer to 320 Fahrenheit for 4 minutes.
3. Put the baking tray in the air fryer and bake at 320 degrees F for 10 minutes or when you see the balls have turned golden brown.
4. Remove the tray and let it cool outside for half an hour and serve.

Brown Butter Cookies

Servings: 6   **15 minutes**

INGREDIENTS

- 2 eggs, whisked.
- 1.5 cups butter.
- 2 cups brown sugar.
- 2/3 cup pecans, chopped.
- 3 cups flour.
- 1 teaspoon baking soda.
- 2 teaspoons vanilla extract.
- 1/2 teaspoon baking powder.

DIRECTIONS

1. Heat up a pan, add butter and cook over medium heat, stir until it melts, add brown sugar and stir until this dissolves.
2. Mix flour with pecans, vanilla extract, baking powder, baking soda, and eggs in a bowl, and stir well.
3. Add brown butter, stir well and arrange spoonfuls of this mix on a lined baking sheet that fits your air fryer.
4. Introduce in the fryer and cook at 340 degrees F for 10 minutes.
5. Leave cookies to cool down and serve.

Pignoli Cookies

Servings: 30   25 minutes

INGREDIENTS

- 10 oz almond paste
- 2 cups pine nuts
- 1/2 cup sugar
- 1 cup confectioners' sugar
- 4 large egg whites, divided
- flour, for shaping dough

DIRECTIONS

1. In a bowl, beat the almond paste and sugar until combined. Then add two egg whites into the almond mixture, mix well.
2. Gradually add the confectioners' sugar to the almond mixture and mix thoroughly to make dough.
3. In second bowl, whisk the remaining two egg whites until the egg whites are foamy.
4. Check the dough by dip your fingers into the flour to keep the dough from sticking to your fingers. Shape the dough into 1-in balls, dip the balls into the egg whites, and coat each ball in the pine nuts.
5. Put the balls in an air fryer lined with baking paper and flatten each ball slightly
6. Baking at 325 degrees F for 18 minutes. Flip the other side of the cookies while baking (9 mins). Leave cookies to cool down and serve.

Pumpkin Cookies

Servings: 24   25 minutes

INGREDIENTS

- 1/4 cup honey.
- 2.5 cups flour.
- 2 tablespoons butter.
- 1/2 teaspoon baking soda.
- 1 tablespoon flax seed, ground.
- 3 tablespoons water.
- 1/2 cup pumpkin flesh, mashed.
- 1/2 cup dark chocolate chips.
- 1 teaspoon vanilla extract.

DIRECTIONS

1. Mix flax seed with water in a bowl, stir and leave aside for a few minutes.
2. In second bowl, mix flour with salt and baking soda.
3. In a third bowl, mix honey with pumpkin puree, butter, vanilla extract and flaxseed.
4. Combine flour with honey mix and chocolate chips and stir.
5. Scoop 1 tablespoon of cookie dough on a lined baking sheet that fits your air fryer, repeat with the rest of the dough, introduce them in your air fryer and cook at 330 degrees F for 18 minutes.
6. Leave cookies to cool down and serve.

Tasty Orange Cookies

Servings: 8   20 minutes

INGREDIENTS

- 1 egg, whisked.
- 2 cups flour.
- 3/4 cup sugar.
- 1 teaspoon baking powder.
- 1/2 cup butter, soft.
- 1 tablespoon orange zest, grated.
- 1 teaspoon vanilla extract.

For the filling:
- 4 ounces cream cheese, soft.
- 2 cups powdered sugar.
- 1/2 cup butter.

DIRECTIONS

1. Mix cream cheese with 1/2 cup butter and 2 cups powdered sugar in a bowl, stir well using your mixer and leave aside for now.
2. In second bowl, mix flour with baking powder.
3. In another bowl, mix 1/2 cup butter with 3/4 cup sugar, egg, vanilla extract and orange zest and whisk well.
4. Combine flour with orange mix, stir well and scoop 1 tablespoon of the mix on a lined baking sheet that fits your air fryer.
5. Repeat with the rest of the orange batter, introduce in the fryer and cook at 340 degrees F for 12 minutes.
6. Leave cookies to cool down, spread cream filling on half of them top with the other cookies and serve.

Chocolate Chip Cookies

INGREDIENTS

- 1/2 cup unsalted butter, softened
- 1/3 cup granulated sugar
- 1/3 cup light brown sugar
- 1 large egg
- 1/2 tsp. vanilla extract
- 1 cup plus 1 tbsp. flour
- 1/2 tsp. baking powder
- 1/4 tsp. baking soda
- 1/2 tsp salt
- 1/4 cup semisweet chocolate chips
- 1/4 cup milk chocolate chips
- 1/4 cup white chocolate chips
- 1/2 cup chopped & toasted walnut pieces

DIRECTIONS

1. Whip together the butter, granulated sugar, and brown sugar using an electric mixer. Add the egg and vanilla and mix well.
2. In another bowl, combine the flour, baking powder, baking soda, and salt. Slowly mix the dry mixture into the butter mixture until creamy.
3. Add all the chocolate chips and walnut pieces to the mixture and mix. Refrigerate the dough for 1 hr.
4. Shape the dough into 1-in balls, Put the balls in an air fryer lined with baking paper and flatten each ball slightly.
5. Baking at 325 degrees F for 18 minutes. Flip the other side of the cookies while baking (9 mins).
6. Let the cookies cool before serving.

Lentils Cookies

Servings: 36   25 minutes

INGREDIENTS

- 1 egg.
- 1 cup water.
- 1 cup white flour.
- 1 cup canned lentils, drained and mashed.
- 1 teaspoon baking powder.
- 1 teaspoon cinnamon powder.
- 1 cup whole wheat flour.
- 1/2 teaspoon nutmeg, ground.
- 1 cup butter, soft.
- 1/2 cup white sugar.
- 1/2 cup brown sugar.
- 2 teaspoons almond extract.
- 1 cup raisins.
- 1 cup rolled oats.
- 1 cup coconut, unsweetened and shredde.

DIRECTIONS

1. Mix white and whole wheat flour with salt, cinnamon, baking powder and nutmeg in a bowl and stir.
2. In second bowl, mix butter with white and brown sugar and stir using your kitchen mixer for 2 minutes.
3. Add egg, almond extract, lentils mix, flour mix, oats, raisins and coconut and stir everything well.
4. Scoop tablespoons of dough on a lined baking sheet that fits your air fryer, introduce them in the fryer and cook at 350 degrees F for 18 minutes.
5. Arrange cookies on a serving platter and serve.

Lentils and Dates Brownies

Servings: 8   25 minutes

INGREDIENTS

- 4 tablespoons almond butter.
- 1 banana, peeled and chopped.
- 28 ounces canned lentils, rinsed and drained.
- 12 dates.
- 1 tablespoon honey.
- 1/2 teaspoon baking soda.
- 2 tablespoons cocoa powder.

DIRECTIONS

1. Mix lentils with butter, banana, cocoa, baking soda, honey in your food processor and blend really well.
2. Add dates, pulse a few more times, pour this into a greased pan that fits your air fryer, spread evenly.
3. Introduce in the fryer at 360 degrees F and bake for 17 minutes.
4. Take brownies mix out of the oven, cut, arrange on a platter and serve.

Vanilla Brownies

 Servings: 8   20 minutes

INGREDIENTS

- 1/2 cup condensed milk
- 1 tbsp unsalted butter (softened or melted).
- 3 tbsp vanilla essence
- 2 tbsp water
- 1/2 cup chopped nuts (use mixed nuts if you prefer)
- 2 cups all-purpose flour (split it up as half a cup, 2 tbsp and 1 tsp)

DIRECTIONS

1. Mix the ingredients together and beat until you get a smooth mixture.
2. Grease tin with butter, Preheat fryer to 300 degrees F for five minutes.
3. Pour batter into tin and place in preheated air fryer, bake at 300 degrees F for 5 minutes. Check that the brownies are done with a knife or toothpick and remove the tray.
4. When the macaroons have cooled, cut them and serve with a scoop of ice cream.

Fudgy Gluten-Free Brownies

INGREDIENTS

- 1 egg.
- 1 egg yolk.
- 1/2 cup almond flour.
- 1/4 tsp salt..
- 1/4 cup unsalted butter.
- 1/4 cup cocoa powder (approx)
- 1/4 tsp baking powder.
- 1/2 cup granulated sugar.
- 1.5 oz unsweetened baker's chocolate, finely chopped.
- 1/2 tsp vanilla extract.

Servings: 4   45 minutes

DIRECTIONS

1. Sift together almond flour, cocoa powder, baking powder and salt in a large bowl
2. Melt the chopped chocolate and butter over medium heat, stirring occasionally. Remove from heat. Add in sugar, stir, let cool slightly. Then Stir in egg and egg yolk until well combined. Stir in vanilla. Fold in almond flour mixture until combined.
3. Pour into 6 silicone square baking cups. Place in bowl of air fryer. Cook on dual heat mode setting with air fryer in the level position for 10-15 minutes or until only a few moist crumbs adhere to toothpick when inserted into center of brownie.
4. Let cool completely. Dust with cocoa powder before serving.

PIE, BISCUITS, TARTS & MORE

Strawberry Pie

🍴 Servings: 12   🕒 30 minutes

INGREDIENTS

For the crust:
- 1 cup coconut, shredded.
- 1 cup sunflower seeds.
- 1/4 cup butter.

For the filling:
- 1/2 cup heavy cream.
- 1 teaspoon gelatin.
- 1/2 tablespoon lemon juice.
- 4 ounces strawberries.
- 8 ounces cream cheese.
- 2 tablespoons water.
- 1/4 teaspoon stevia.
- 8 ounces strawberries, chopped for serving.

DIRECTIONS

1. Mix sunflower seeds with coconut, a pinch of salt and butter in your food processor, pulse and press this on the bottom of a cake pan that fits your air fryer.
2. Heat up a pan with the water over medium heat, add gelatin, stir until it dissolves, leave aside to cool down, add this to your food processor, mix with 4 ounces strawberries, cream cheese, lemon juice and stevia and blend well.
3. Add heavy cream, stir well and spread this over crust.
4. Top with 8 ounces strawberries, introduce in your air fryer and cook at 330 degrees F for 15-18 minutes.
5. Keep in the fridge until serve

Pumpkin Pie

Servings: 6   25 minutes

INGREDIENTS

- 1 tablespoon sugar.
- 2 tablespoons water.
- 1 tablespoon butter.
- 2 tablespoons flour.

For the pumpkin pie filling:
- 3.5 ounces pumpkin flesh, chopped.
- 1 egg, whisked.
- 1 teaspoon mixed spice.
- 1 tablespoon sugar.
- 1 teaspoon nutmeg.
- 3 ounces water.

DIRECTIONS

1. Put 3 ounces water in a pot, bring to a boil over medium heat, add pumpkin, egg, 1 tablespoon sugar, spice and nutmeg, stir, boil for 20 minutes, take off heat.
2. Blend the above mixture in a blender.
3. Mix flour with butter, 1 tablespoon sugar and 2 tablespoons water in a bowl and knead your dough well.
4. Grease a pie pan that fits your air fryer with butter, Put dough into the pan, fill with pumpkin pie filling, place in your air fryer's basket and bake at 360 degrees F for 15-18 minutes.
5. Slice and serve warm.

Coconut Hand Pies

INGREDIENTS

The Pie Crust:
- 450 grams All purpose flour, plus extra for dusting.
- 1 tsp Salt.
- 225 grams Unsalted butter, cube, cold.
- 6 tbsp Ice cold water.

The Coconut Cream Filling:
- 1/4 cup Sugar.
- 1/2 cup Shredded fresh coconut
- 2 tbsp Cornstarch.
- 1/4 tsp Salt.
- 1.5 cups Coconut milk, heated to a simmer.
- 2 pcs Egg yolks.
- 2 tbsp Unsalted butter.
- 1 tsp Vanilla.

6 Pies | 20 minutes

DIRECTIONS

To make the coconut cream filling:
In your Instant Pot, whisk in the pot the sugar, cornstarch, and salt. Pour the hot coconut milk into the sugar mixture. Keep whisking until the mixture boils and thickens slightly. Add the egg yolks and continue whisking. Remove from the inner pot and pour mixture into a bowl, then stir in the butter and vanilla, cool to room temperature. Stir in the fresh coconut shreds. Cover and refrigerate before use.

1. Put the flour and salt into the processor and pulse a few times to combine.
2. Distribute butter cubes on top of the flour. Pulse several times until the mixture resembles large pea-sized crumbs and changes to a darker color. Take a bit of the mixture and pinch together with your fingers; if it holds together, dough is ready for the water.
3. Remove the processor lid cap and slowly drizzle in the ice cold water while pulsing, until the mixture just starts to form a ball.
4. Dust work surface with flour. Transfer the dough mixture on and shape into a rough cohesive ball. Flatten the ball into a 1 inch thick disc. Wrap dough in plastic wrap and refrigerate for 30 minutes.
5. Let it thaw before rolling out. Roll out the dough on a flour surface. Cut 5-inch circles using a cookie cutter.
6. Place coconut pie filling on the bottom half of the crust. Moisten the outside edges of the pie crust with water. Fold the dough over the filling to form half moons. Pinch the edges of the crust together.
7. In a small bowl, mix together 1 egg and 1 tsp water. Brush the pies with egg was all oven the tops. Sprinkle 1/2 tsp sugar over each pie. Slice three slits in the top side of the pie crusts.
8. Preheat the Air Fryer to 180oC.
9. Place the pies in the Air Fryer basket and bake for 10 minutes, turning pies half way through cooking time.

Chicken Pie

Servings: 4   30 minutes

INGREDIENTS

- 2 chicken thighs, boneless, skinless and cubed.
- 1 carrot, chopped.
- 1 teaspoon Worcestershire sauce.
- 1 yellow onion, chopped.
- 2 potatoes, chopped.
- 1 tablespoon butter, melted.
- 1 teaspoon soy sauce.
- 1 teaspoon Italian seasoning.
- ½ teaspoon garlic powder.
- 2 mushrooms, chopped.
- 1 tablespoon flour.
- 1 tablespoon milk.
- 2 puff pastry sheets.
- Salt and black pepper to the taste.

DIRECTIONS

1. Heat a pan over medium heat, add the potatoes, onions and carrots to the pan, stir and cook for 2 minutes.
2. Add chicken and mushrooms, pepper, salt, garlic powder, soy sauce, Italian seasoning, Worcestershire sauce, flour and milk, stir really well and take off heat.
3. Place 1 puff pastry sheet on the bottom of your air fryer's pan and trim edge excess.
4. Add the chicken mixture created in step 1 and 2, then top with the other puff pastry sheet, trim excess as well and brush pie with butter.
5. Place in your air fryer and cook at 360 degrees F for 6-8 minutes.
6. Leave pie to cool down, slice and serve.

Ham Breakfast Pie

Servings: 6   30 minutes

INGREDIENTS

- 16 ounces crescent rolls dough.
- 2 cups ham, cooked and chopped.
- 2 eggs, whisked.
- 2 cups cheddar cheese, grated 1 tablespoon parmesan, grated.
- Salt and black pepper to the taste.
- Cooking spray.

DIRECTIONS

1. Grease your air fryer's pan with cooking spray and press half of the crescent rolls dough on the bottom.
2. Mix eggs with cheddar cheese, parmesan, salt and pepper in a bowl, beat well and add over dough.
3. Spread ham, cut the rest of the crescent rolls dough in strips, arrange them over ham and cook at 300 degrees F for 23- 25 minutes.
4. Slice pie and serve.

Peach Pie

Servings: 4   40 minutes

INGREDIENTS

- 1 pie dough.
- 2 tablespoons butter, melted.
- 2.25 pounds peaches, pitted and chopped.
- 1/2 cup sugar.
- 2 tablespoons cornstarch.
- A pinch of nutmeg, ground.
- 2 tablespoons flour.
- 1 tablespoon dark rum.
- 1 tablespoon lemon juice.

DIRECTIONS

1. Mix peaches with cornstarch, sugar, flour, nutmeg, rum, lemon juice and butter in a bowl and stir well.
2. Roll pie dough into a pie pan that fits your air fryer and press well.
3. Pour and spread mixture in step 1 into pie pan, introduce in your air fryer and bake at 350 degrees F for 35 minutes.
4. Serve warm or cold.

Mini Apple Pies

INGREDIENTS

- 1 egg
- 1 medium apple, peeled & diced
- 1 tablespoon unsalted butter
- 2.5 tablespoons granulated sugar
- 1 teaspoon milk
- 1/2 teaspoon ground cinnamon
- 1/2 teaspoon ground allspice
- 1/2 teaspoon ground nutmeg
- 1 sheet pre-made pie dough

Servings: 3   40 minutes

DIRECTIONS

1. Mix the diced apples in the granulated sugar, butter, cinnamon, nutmeg and pepper in a saucepan, stirring, over low heat. Cook for 2 minutes and then turn off the heat.
2. Bring the pot of apple mixture to cool at room temperature for 30 minutes.
3. Cut the pie dough into two to three 5-inch circles. Add the apple filling to the center of each pie dough circle and use your finger to apply water to the outer ends. Then crimp the dough shut and cut a small slit on the top.
4. Mix together the egg and milk to make an egg wash, and brush it on the top of each pie.
5. Put the pies into the preheated air fryer, bake for 350°F in 10 minutes.
6. Remove when pies are golden brown, then let the pie cool and serve.

Cinnamon Sugar Churros
with Dark Chocolate Dipping Sauce

INGREDIENTS

- 2 eggs
- 1/4 cup butter, cubed
- 1/4 tsp salt
- 1/2 cup all-purpose flour
- 1 tsp ground cinnamon
- 1/2 cup 35% heavy cream
- 1 tbsp vegetable oil
- 1/2 cup dark chocolate, finely chopped
- 2 tbsp maple syrup
- 1/4 cup granulated sugar

Servings: 4   45 minutes

DIRECTIONS

1. In saucepan set over medium heat, bring 1/2 cup water, add butter and salt to boil. Remove saucepan from heat. Using wooden spoon, add flour, stir well.
2. Continue to heat the pan on the stove, stirring constantly, for 2-4 minutes or until the mixture coats the pan with a thin film. Remove from heat; stir for about 5 minutes or until cooled slightly.
3. Beat in eggs, one at a time, beating well after each addition until pastry dough is shiny and smooth.
4. Scoop the dough into an ice cream bag with a large star tip. Using 3-inch ring mold, shape the churro. Oil drizzle on top. Then place them in the greased tray of the air fryer. Bake at 330 degrees F for 12 to 15 minutes or until golden brown.
5. Meanwhile, in a small saucepan set over medium heat, heat the cream until just beginning to boil; pour in the chocolate. Let stand for 1 minute; beat until smooth. Stir in maple syrup.
6. Stir in sugar and cinnamon. Sprinkle churros in cinnamon sugar and serve with chocolate sauce for dipping.

Cheese Crackers

Servings: 15   25 minutes

INGREDIENTS

- 1 pound cream cheese.
- 2 tablespoons butter.
- 1/2 teaspoon vanilla extract.
- 4 tablespoons sugar.
- 2 eggs.
- 1 cup graham crackers, crumbled.

DIRECTIONS

1. Mix crackers with butter in a bowl.
2. Put crackers mix on the bottom of a lined cake pan, introduce in your air fryer and cook at 350 degrees F for 4 minutes.
3. Meanwhile, in another bowl, mix sugar with cream cheese, eggs and vanilla and whisk well.
4. Spread filling over crackers crust and bake your cheese crackers in your air fryer at 310 degrees F for 15 minutes.
5. Leave crackers in the fridge for 3 hours and serve.

Mushrooms Stuffed
with Choriz

Servings: 16   30 minutes

INGREDIENTS

- 1/2 cup goat cheese, softened.
- 3 tbsp Parmesan cheese grated.
- 16 cremini mushrooms
- 1 tbsp olive oil.
- 1 tbsp fresh thyme, finely chopped.
- 1 tbsp balsamic vinegar.
- 1 clove garlic, minced.
- 1/4 tsp chili pepper flakes.
- 1/3 cup cured chorizo sausage, finely chopped.
- 2 tbsp sun-dried tomatoes, finely chopped.

DIRECTIONS

1. Mash together goat cheese, Parmesan, thyme, vinegar and garlic.
2. Stir in chorizo, sun-dried tomatoes and chili flakes.
3. Add 2 spoons of the chorizo mixture sautéed in step 2 to the mushrooms.
4. Put mushrooms on the rack in bowl of air fryer. Drizzle with oil. Cook on dual heat mode setting with air fryer in the level position for 10 to 12 minutes or until mushrooms are tender and topping is golden brown.

Alternatively, you can replace the cremini with white button mushrooms.

Cheddar Biscuits

Servings: 8   20 minutes

INGREDIENTS

- 2.3 cup self-rising flour.
- 1 cup flour.
- 1/2 cup + 1 tablespoon butter, melted.
- 1/2 cup cheddar cheese, grated.
- 2 tablespoons sugar.
- 1.3 cup buttermilk.

DIRECTIONS

1. Mix self-rising flour with 1/2 cup butter, sugar, cheddar cheese and buttermilk in a bowl, and stir until you obtain a dough.
2. Spread 1 cup flour out a surface, roll dough, flatten it, cut 8 circles with a cookie cutter and coat them with flour.
3. Line air fryer's basket with tin foil, add biscuits, brush them with melted butter and cook them at 380 degrees F for 20 minutes.
4. Enjoy!

Biscuits Casserole
with Sausage

Servings: 8 25 minutes

INGREDIENTS

- 12 ounces biscuits, quartered.
- A pinch of salt and black pepper.
- 3 tablespoons flour
- 2.5 cups milk
- ½ pound sausage, chopped.
- Cooking spray.

DIRECTIONS

1. Mix softened butter with sugar, vanilla and cinnamon and beat well in a bowl.
2. Spread this on bread slices, place them in your air fryer and cook at 400 degrees F for 4-5 minutes.
3. Divide among plates and serve.

Buttermilk Biscuits

Servings: 4 25 minutes

INGREDIENTS

- 1.25 cup white flour.
- 1 teaspoon sugar.
- ½ cup self-rising flour.
- ¼ teaspoon baking soda.
- ¾ cup buttermilk Maple syrup for serving.
- ½ teaspoon baking powder.
- 4 tablespoons butter, cold and cubed+ 1 tablespoon melted butter.

DIRECTIONS

1. Mix white flour with self-rising flour, baking soda, baking powder and sugar and stir in a bowl.
2. Add cold butter to the bowl and stir well with the above mixture.
3. Add buttermilk, stir until you obtain a dough and transfer to a floured surface.
4. Roll your dough and cut 10 pieces using a round cutter.
5. Arrange biscuits in your air fryer's cake pan, brush them with melted butter and cook at 400 degrees F for 8 minutes.
6. Serve them for breakfast with some maple syrup on top.

Simple Potato Chips

🍴 Servings: 4   🕐 30 minutes

INGREDIENTS

- 4 potatoes, scrubbed, peeled into thin chips, soaked in water for 30 minutes, drained and pat dried.
- 2 teaspoons rosemary, chopped.
- 1 tablespoon olive oil.
- Salt the taste.

DIRECTIONS

1. Mix potato chips with salt and oil in a bowl.
2. Preheat the air fryer at 250 degrees F in 3 minutes.
3. Place them in your air fryer's basket and cook at 330 degrees F for 30 minutes.
4. Divide among plates, sprinkle rosemary all over and serve as a side dish.

Sweet Potato Chips
in Green Goddess Sauce

Servings: 4   20 minutes

INGREDIENTS

- 2 pcs Sweet potatoes, sliced thinly.
- 1 tbsp Coconut oil.
- 1/2 tsp Salt.
- 2 tbsp Light brown sugar.
- 2 tsp Chili powder.

For the green goddess dip:
- 1/2 pc Avocado, peeled.
- 1/2 cup Greek yogurt.
- 1 tsp Dijon mustard.
- 1/2 tsp Salt.
- 1/4 cup Fresh mint.
- 1/3 cup Fresh parsley.
- 1/4 cup Fresh chives.
- 1/4 cup Fresh basil.

DIRECTIONS

1. Preheat the Instant Air Fryer to 180oC in 10 minutes
2. Toss the sliced sweet potatoes in a bowl of coconut oil.
3. Add the chips in the Air Fryer and shake gently the basket/tray from time to time as they cook.
4. Meanwhile, make the dip. Blend all ingredients for the dip in a food processor until smooth.
5. Add the sugar, salt and chilli powder in the bowl and toss the chips again.
6. Serve the chips with the green goddess dip.

Tasty Cinnamon Toast

Servings: 6   15 minutes

INGREDIENTS

- 1 stick butter, soft.
- 1.5 tsp cinnamon powder.
- 1.5 tsp vanilla extract.
- 12 bread slices.
- 1/2 cup sugar.

DIRECTIONS

1. Mix softened butter with sugar, vanilla and cinnamon and beat well in a bowl.
2. Spread this on bread slices, place them in your air fryer and cook at 400 degrees F for 4-5 minutes.
3. Divide among plates and serve.

Strawberry Jam Tarts

Servings: 9   18 minutes

INGREDIENTS

- Strawberry Jam Water
- 100g Butter
- 225g Plain Flour
- 25g Caster Sugar

DIRECTIONS

1. Mix sugar, flour, and butter in a large bowl. Then rub the fat into the sugar and flour until the mixture resembles breadcrumbs.
2. Add water until you have a soft dough.
3. Grease the bottom and sides of the mini cake pan, pour the batter into the cake pan, top with 2 teaspoons of strawberry (or raspberry) jam, and place in the preheated air fryer. Cook for 10 minutes at 180 degrees Celsius or until the cake is cooked through.
4. Take out the cake to cool and serve.

Chocolate Tarts

Servings: 8   25 minutes

INGREDIENTS

- 1.5 cup plain flour
- 2 cups cold water
- 1/2 cup cocoa powder.
- 2 tbsp powdered sugar
- 3 tbsp unsalted butter
- 1 tbsp sliced cashew

For Truffle filling:
- 3 tbsp butter
- 1.5 melted chocolate
- 1 cup fresh cream

DIRECTIONS

1. Mix the flour, butter, cocoa powder and sugar in a large bowl, . The mixture should resemble breadcrumbs. Knead the dough using the cold milk and wrap it and leave it to cool for 10 minutes.
2. Roll the dough out into the pie and prick the sides of the pie.
3. Mix the ingredients for the filling in another bowl. Make sure that it is a little thick. Add the filling to the pie and cover it with the second round. Put pie into the tin,
4. Preheat the fryer to 300 Fahrenheit for 4 minutes. Put the tin in the basket and cover it. bake at 300 Fahrenheit in 8 minutes. When the pastry has turned golden brown, you will need to remove the tin and let it cool. Cut into slices and serve with a dollop of cream.

Blueberry Tarts

Servings: 10   25 minutes

INGREDIENTS

- 2 tbsp powdered sugar
- 1.5 cup plain flour
- 3 tbsp unsalted butter
- 1 tbsp sliced cashew
- 2 cups cold water

For filling:

- 3 tbsp butter
- 1 cup fresh cream
- 1 cup fresh blueberries (Sliced)

DIRECTIONS

1. Mix well the ingredients together to form a crumbly mixture. Knead the mixture with cold milk and wrap it.
2. Roll the dough into two large circles and place the dough in the cake pan and poke the edges of the dough with a fork.
3. Heat the filling ingredients over low heat and pour over the dough in the tin. Then cover pie tin with the second round.
4. Preheat the fryer to 300 Fahrenheit for 4 minutes. Put the tin in the basket and cover it. bake at 300 Fahrenheit in 8 minutes. When the pastry has turned golden brown, you will need to remove the tin and let it cool. Cut into slices and serve with a dollop of cream.

Fruit Tarts

Servings: 8   30 minutes

INGREDIENTS

- 3 tbsp unsalted butter
- 1.5 cup plain flour
- 2 cups cold water
- 1/2 cup cocoa powder
- 1 tbsp sliced cashew
- 2 tbsp powdered sugar

For Truffle filling:
- 3 tbsp butter
- 2 cups mixed sliced fruits
- 1 cup fresh cream

DIRECTIONS

1. Mix all the ingredients together using milk into dough that is soft. Roll the dough out and cut into two circles. Press the dough into the pie tins and prick on all sides using a fork.
2. In a bowl, mix the ingredients for the filling. Make sure that it is a little thick. Add the filling to the pie and cover it with the second round.
3. Preheat the fryer to 300 Fahrenheit for 4 minutes. Put the tin in the basket and cover it, bake at 300 Fahrenheit in 8 minutes . When the pastry has turned golden brown, you will need to remove the tin and let it cool. Cut into slices and serve with a dollop of cream.

Lemon Tart

🍴 Servings: 6   🕐 35 minutes

INGREDIENTS

For the crust:
- 2 cups white flour.
- 2 tablespoons sugar.
- 12 tablespoons cold butter.
- 3 tablespoons ice water.
- A pinch of salt.

For the filling:
- 2 eggs, whisked.
- Juice from 2 lemons.
- Zest from 2 lemons, grated.
- 1.25 cup sugar.
- 10 tablespoons melted and chilled butter.

DIRECTIONS

1. Mix 2 cups flour with a pinch of salt and 2 tablespoons sugar in a bowl and whisk.
2. Add 12 tablespoons butter and the water, knead until you obtain a dough, shape a ball, wrap in foil and keep in the fridge for 1 hour.
3. Transfer dough to a floured surface, flatten it, arrange on the bottom of a tart pan, prick with a fork, keep in the fridge for 20 minutes, introduce in your air fryer at 360 degrees F and bake for 15 minutes.
4. In another bowl, mix 1.25 cup sugar with eggs, 10 tablespoons butter, lemon juice and lemon zest and whisk very well.
5. Pour this into pie crust, spread evenly, introduce in the fryer and cook at 360 degrees F for 20 minutes.
6. Cut and serve.

Blueberry Pop Tart

Servings: 4   45 minutes

INGREDIENTS

For Dough:
- 20g Almond Flour
- 70g All Purpose Flour
- 24g PB Party Protein Cookie Butter Powder
- 45g Whey/Casein Blend Vanilla Protein Powder
- 140g Plain Nonfat Greek Yogurt
- 8g Zero Cal Sweetener of your choice.

For Filling:
- 20g Blueberry Preserves per Pop Tart (regular jam or smashing up berries on your own)

For Frosting:
- 32g Protein Cheesecake Frosting per Pop Tart

Blueberry Pop Tart

DIRECTIONS

- 1. Mix your dry dough ingredients into a food processor and beat until combined. Then add your Greek yogurt and blend on slow until there's a dough ball. Take the dough ball and put it in a bowl and then place it in the freezer to cool for 20-30 minutes.

- 2. Then the dough is done cooling, lay a silicone rolling mat and cover the whole surface with flour to ensure sticking doesn't occur.

- 3. Take 1/3rd of dough and roll it in the flour on the mat. Use the rolling pin to roll out the dough as much as you can. Once there is a large piece of dough rolled out, use the cutter and slice out a rectangle pop tart shaped piece of dough. This will be the mold for the other pieces.

- 4. Lay down one of the pieces of dough and add filling (leave 1/3 for the icing on top of the pop tart) to the middle leaving at least an 1/2 inch around the edges so you can pinch the pop tart shut with the top piece. Add the rest of the filling/frosting to the fridge to keep it cool.

- 5. Brush on egg white wash around the edges where the filling is not. Then add the top piece of dough and press the edges shut. Add more egg white wash on top covering the whole pop tart. Press the edges shut and cut off the uneven edges with a pizza cutter. Crimp edges with a fork and poke holes in the top so the pop tart can breathe in the oven and doesn't explode.

- 6. Baking at 360 degrees F for 8 minutes. Carefully flip the pop tarts after 5 minutes. Then once done, carefully take out and add to a cooling rack. Use a fork to re-poke holes in the top to get the extra air out. Once cool, add desired toppings and enjoy!

Plum and Currant Tart

Servings: 6   45 minutes

INGREDIENTS

For the crumble:
- 3 tablespoons milk.
- 1 cup brown rice flour
- 1/4 cup almond flour.
- 1/4 cup millet flour.
- 1/2 cup cane sugar.
- 10 tablespoons butter, soft.

For the filling:
- 1 cup white currants.
- 1 pound small plums, pitted and halved.
- 1/4 teaspoon ginger powder.
- 2 tablespoons cornstarch.
- 1 teaspoon lime juice.
- 3 tablespoons sugar.
- 1/2 teaspoon vanilla extract.
- 1/2 teaspoon cinnamon powder.

DIRECTIONS

1. Mix brown rice flour with 1/2 cup sugar, millet flour, almond flour, butter and milk in a bowl and stir until you obtain a sand like dough.
2. Reserve 1/4 of the dough, press the rest of the dough into a tart pan that fits your air fryer and keep in the fridge for 30 minutes.
3. Meanwhile, in a bowl, mix plums with currants, 3 tablespoons sugar, cornstarch, vanilla extract, cinnamon, ginger and lime juice and stir well.
4. Pour this over tart crust, crumble reserved dough on top, introduce in your air fryer and cook at 350 degrees F for 35 minutes.
5. Leave tart to cool down and serve.

Printed in Great Britain
by Amazon